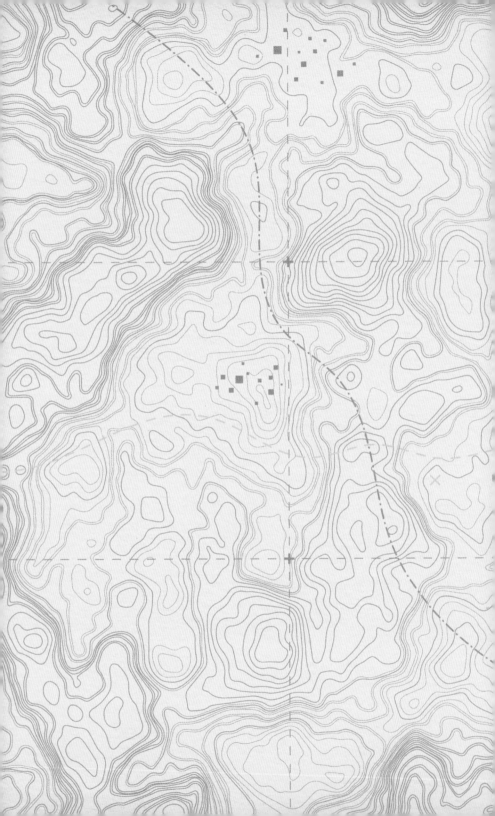

Here's what people are saying about *Blue Skies*:

"James, like all of us, has been on an exciting, life-changing journey all of his life. In this heartwarming book, he shares his unique story with keen insight, humor, and grace. He'll inspire you to launch out and see what God has waiting for you, just around the corner."

—DR. RICHARD BLACKABY
President of Blackaby Ministries International,
Co-author of *Experiencing God*

"When James Barnett steps into a room, joy enters with him. In the stories told in Blue Skies, you find out why ... if you choose God's perspective, life is an adventure full of surprising joy. Don't miss what God has for you!"

—CHERYL BACHELDER
Former CEO, Popeyes Louisiana Kitchen, Inc. | Author of *Dare to Serve*

"James Barnett is a man who loves people and Jesus, asking good questions and telling great stories, looking for the divine in ordinary moments and in extraordinary adventures. Through his words, he'll help you do all of those things in your life too. Let this book be your travel guide to new places of faith, hope, and wonder."

—HOLLEY GERTH
Wall Street Journal Bestselling Author and Life Coach

"James is one of my favorite people on earth. The joy he expresses in this book is reflective of the same man I have known for over a decade. He is positive, inspiring, humble, and vulnerable. His heart is filled with love for family, for others, and his Lord. You'll love his life's journey as described in these pages, but even more so you'll appreciate the vital spiritual lesson to see God in everything around us and to pay attention to all that life has to offer."

—SCOTT MACLELLAN
CEO of TouchPoint Support Services

"When we look at the events of our lives from God's perspective instead of our own, everything changes. In Blue Skies, James really challenges the typical inward-looking thinking so prevalent in American life. Real encouragement can be found seeing all that God accomplishes in our lives every day."

—RAY HENDRICKSON
President | CEO, Christianbook

"With everything going on in our world today, we need a book that is uplifting. Blue Skies reminds us of keeping the right perspective and counting our blessings. James takes us through his faith journey while sharing his trips across our nation discovering its beauty. The images he creates in our minds reinforce his optimism. I especially appreciate his view about seeking what God is up to every day. This perspective creates positive expectations and excitement, as He reveals His plan for our lives."

—DR. ELI JONES
Thought Leader. Author. Professor. Believer.
Author of *Run Toward Your Goliaths*

"For the past decade, I have witnessed and personally walked alongside James Barnett as he faced incredible challenges in business and family—some might say, insurmountable, faith-debilitating trials. Through it all, he would always say, "I don't understand, but I know God must have a plan." James is a Blue Sky leader whose faith, perseverance, creativity, and hard work has resulted in human flourishing for all within his sphere of influence. Listen well, there is gold in his story!"

—DR. RICHARD S. LYTLE
President & Chief Executive Officer, CEO Forum

"For every emerging visionary leader seeking direction, endurance and substance, James' wisdom is like a compass guiding you into the future that has been waiting for you. In Blue Skies, you'll learn to turn frustration into focus and obstacles into optimism. A must read!"

—MARSHAWN EVANS DANIELS
Godfidence Coach® | TV Personality | Reinvention Strategist for Women,
Founder of SheProfits.com

"This book by my friend, James Barnett, is a wondrous treat! Blue Skies is a book of God's awe and wonder laced with spiritual and leadership lessons that will change your perspective. My take-away: even with life's challenges . . . blue skies will always break through."

—SQuire Rushnell
Producer | Writer | Author of The Godwinks books

"What do you get when you mix a passion for God and love of people into daily living? You'll find out in Blue Skies as James Barnett reveals through his own life how living our way doesn't compare with living the adventures of faith in God's bigger purpose and plan."

—LISA STILWELL
Author of *100 Days of Faith Over Fear*

"*Looking back at his humble beginnings (arguably the best kind!!), James takes the reader on a journey to take the ordinary into the extraordinary, the mundane details of life into the much wider, God-perspective. With his keen mind of relived, travel-log adventures, James shows the reader that life is a classroom of rich experiences and for those who can see it (or hear it), God still speaks.*"

—DR. ROBERT CUPP
Founding Pastor of Fellowship Bible Church of Northwest Arkansas

"*James offers us a travel journal from his life to help us see how God travels with us in our lives. He describes illuminating experiences from his family's trips to the national parks to reflect on how he has sought to align his business career, his family life, and his friendships to conform with God's perspective on life. It is a book filled with joy and sorrow, wisdom and humor, faithfulness, and family.*"

—DR. CHIP POLLARD
President of John Brown University

"*Through memory provoking (or powerful) and whimsical stories, James challenged me to open my eyes and see God at work all around me! He will make you feel like you're a passenger in each of his stories. And then use his 'Questions to Ponder' to challenge you to think differently about God and your life. A fun read with life-impacting perspectives!*"

—DAVID ROTH
President & CEO, Workmatters

"*James is challenging us to 'look again' at our life's adventures with an eye to see God's activity. He uses his personal adventures to point out that God is always at work and desires to reveal Himself to us if we would only take time to 'look again.' It is a must-read to bring real meaning and excitement to your next adventure.*"

—STEVE MENEFEE
Retired President, Arrow Electronics

"*As I was reading Blue Skies, I could hear James' voice and see his expressions and mannerisms. It was clear to me that this book was from his heart. I've known him for many years and I can tell you that this book is written by a man of integrity who is a great leader. You will love the stories about his travels and the connections to our faith.*"

—DR. MATTHEW A. WALLER
Dean, Sam M. Walton College of Business, University of Arkansas

JAMES BARNETT

BLUE
SKIES

How to Live in Extraordinary
Expectation of What's
Around the Corner

DaySpring

LIVE YOUR FAITH

Published by:

21154 Highway 16 East
Siloam Springs, AR 72761
dayspring.com

Editorial Direction by: Ami McConnell
Co-authored by: Gini Wietecha
Cover Design by: Jessica Wei

Printed in China
Prime: J6787
ISBN: 978-1-64870-289-1

This book is dedicated to the person that wants

to experience an extraordinary and adventurous life.

Take it in! Mark the moment! Live it out!

"No eye has seen, no ear has heard,

no mind has conceived what God has prepared

for those who love Him."

II CORINTHIANS 2:9 NIV

adventure

/ad'ven(t)SHər/

noun

1 an unusual and exciting, typically hazardous experience.

2 daring activity that calls for enthusiasm.

3 exploration of unknown territory.

synonyms

thrill · risk · danger · perilousness · uncertainty ·
pursuit · experience · quest · venture · escapade

For a deeper dive into the stories in *Blue Skies*

including family photos, a small group reading guide, and more,

please scan the QR code below or visit *dayspring.com/blueskies*.

CONTENTS

INTRODUCTION

Let's face it. Life just isn't that exciting most of the time! Everyday life can get you down. Most days feel like work, we have problems, and we can lose track of our real destination.

Life is primarily lived on "the side of the mountain" hiking life's trail. My family and I took some incredible hikes over twelve years of visiting forty-four national parks, and the truth is, very little time was spent "on the mountaintop." We would prepare for months, then rent a van, drive three to four hours a day, hike two to four hours to the summit of a mountain or arch, then get there and say, "Wow! Take it in!"

Twenty minutes later we were hiking back down the mountain, scrambling back into the van, and moving on to the next place. As my daughter, Abbey, would say, "Dad, this is a lot of boring?" And you know what? She was right. But these trips helped me gain perspective—to look again—to see God differently.

We're all busy with "in the meantime" life and need new life experiences to help us gain the right perspective. These trips to national parks helped me see life differently, and I think they will help you too.

God is an awesome God. His creation is amazing! The mountains, the streams, the arches, the lakes, the forests, the color, the oceans, the sunrises and sunsets— all are breathtaking. God is always working and always up to something more, but we'll miss it if we aren't paying attention.

When my dad stepped away from a full-time job at age seventy, he started writing letters. First, he started writing them to his seven children, their spouses, and his grandkids. Then it expanded to other family members and friends. Before long, he was sending letters to more than one hundred people! Over a period of twenty-five years, he wrote more than two hundred letters about life and about every subject you could think of.

When he was seventy-five, he wrote a letter to his seven children that read "When I got old, I thought I wouldn't have so many problems . . . I was wrong!" In the letter, he proceeded to tell us that he had more problems than ever and it was really hard sometimes, but he was learning that God was more than able to help him through those problems and even live with joy "in the meantime." And he encouraged us to do the same.

I was in my thirties at the time, and I didn't quite get it. Since he was not only my dad but also an important mentor, I visited with him all the time. We visited about life's problems and why they happen. There are so many misunderstandings with people, so many health issues, and so many problems in our world.

He shared his experiences, and he encouraged me to not lose hope but keep perspective. He told me how easy it was to lose track of our real destination. I was busy living life and running fast. But I did begin to approach life a little differently after these conversations. I began to look for the "wow" moments of God in ordinary life. I set out to ask different questions. Instead of asking, "Why God?" I started asking, "What, God? . . . What are You up to?" And over time, I came to another question:

What if I started living with excited anticipation of what God is up to next? Would I live differently?

You see, the Bible tells us we were created for a

purpose—for *His* purpose, for a specific time and season—and that God will give us assignments along the way. God is always working. Yes, He is working in the ordinary things of life to do the extraordinary. And He uses people like you and me to do His work.

> *What if I started living with excited anticipation of what God is up to next? Would I live differently?*

Here's the reality: there are always "blue skies" and sunshine even when it's cloudy and we can't see them. Likewise, God is there to bless and encourage you, even when you can't see or feel Him. He loves you and is for you. You are special, you are loved, you are not alone, and you have a purpose.

Many, many years ago, I started saying a morning prayer soon after I woke up. Just lying there in bed, I prayed, "Lord, today You have a plan, and it's not mine. I know You are at work, and I want to join You." Then I would spend my day looking for the answer to "What is God up to next?" and joining Him. Without that prayer and time to meditate on the Lord, I find myself rushing into the day and getting absorbed with its challenges. Before long, I lose perspective.

This prayer centers my heart on His plan and not my plan for the day. Yes, I have a lot to do each day, but I give the Lord complete control to adjust my day to His plan.

My hope is that my story can inspire you to look for God in your everyday life, because once you see Him, you cannot unsee Him. Yes, our stories are different, but our universal need to know and experience God are the same.

As you read through each chapter, my hope is your perspective will change and you'll find that no matter what you're facing today, God has amazing things in store for you just around the corner. He can accomplish infinitely more than we could ever possibly think or imagine (Ephesians 3:20).

He is ready to take you on an exciting adventure! Are you ready to go?

PART ONE

HOW IT ALL STARTED

CHAPTER 1

BEFORE THE ADVENTURE

I'm a sucker for a sunrise.

Sleeping in isn't my style. God wired me to be an early riser. I wake up ready to drink my coffee, and eager to watch the sunrise from a little ridge in the Ozarks, right outside the city limits of Siloam Springs, Arkansas. I've always loved this view. It's a special place. I took my wife here on our second date when it was nothing but a patch of wild sorrel, chickweed, and clover. "Someday I'll build a house up here," I said, trying to impress her. And I did it too. I built her that house—some twenty-five years later. And after all these years, I'm still trying to impress her! Now I get to watch as the sun peaks over the mountains. The birds are singing, and the neighbor's rooster is crowing. Sometimes a deer or two graze nearby. Witnessing God's creation inspires me for the day ahead. It's during this time that I'm especially watching and listening for God's "wow moments."

Then I hop in my Yukon and make my way out into the

big, wide world. Adventure time! Rolling down the small, two-lane, open roads never gets old. Driving toward my next experience—whatever God has for me—revs me up and gets me going, eyes wide open.

But I wasn't always this way. My life has had many ups, downs, roadblocks, and curves, just as God said it would. But I have to say, it's been quite the journey. As a child, I never would have dreamed of the life He had in store for me.

I grew up in a small town, the youngest of seven. My parents were what we used to call "salt-of-the-earth folks" or part of "the greatest generation." They were wonderful people. They worked hard, taught us kids right from wrong, made sure we got a good education, and brought us up to love the Lord. They had their hands full keeping us all fed, but God always provided. My sisters say God multiplied the food by the time it got to the table. We had a big garden, a milk cow, and some chickens, and that kept us going.

This was normal for folks in our area—just good, hardworking, God-fearing people. My dad said he grew up backward, bashful, and poor. But he ended up with so much more. His family lived on a farm by the beautiful ice-cold Little Flint Creek, and they lived off the land. His dad, right alongside my grandma, farmed and cared for the animals, and for a day job, he cut and loaded railroad ties, which he did most of his life. After high school, my dad was drafted and served in WWII. He went to college on a GI Bill and graduated in two and a half years with a biology degree. He taught school, pastored small country churches, and sold stuff on the side, all while raising a family.

My mom was equally amazing. If ever there was a pioneer woman, she was it. She was what we called a "homemaker" in those days, but she was so much more than that. She only stood at five feet, one-half inch but was a woman of purpose and resolve. She was the rock of our home. She not only raised seven kids but also made sure we had everything we needed to succeed. No one believed in us more—we could achieve great things if we loved the Lord and worked hard. While she was always kind and compassionate, no one intimidated her. She always held her head high. Even into her nineties, she served hundreds of needy people. She had a solid, unconditional, and selfless love for others. Few mark the world like she did.

She joyfully partnered with my dad in all his endeavors yet found her own voice and calling in serving others. Her mom and dad were also farmers, but they had an apple and peach orchard. Mom and Dad met in high school; she was fifteen, and he was eighteen. Their first date was on a Saturday night at a "picture show," as my mom used to say.

They were married just over seventy-four years before Dad passed away. They loved life and loved others with a contagious passion. You couldn't help but be inspired by the way they lived, the way they served, and the way they loved.

HUMBLE BEGINNINGS: WORKING FOR DONUTS

My dad's older brother, Ervie, owned and operated one of the first drive-ins and places to "eat out" in Siloam Springs, Arkansas. It was a 1950s drive-in with a menu offering every boy's favorites: hot dogs, chili cheese dogs, juicy hamburgers and cheeseburgers, fresh-cut french fries, and twenty flavors of the creamiest milkshakes you've ever tasted. But you can't serve hamburgers for breakfast, so Uncle Ervie came up with a fantastic idea: transform his drive-in into a donut shop every morning.

Now, these were not your average donuts. No, these were out-of-this-world donuts. They were freshly made cake donuts, covered in cherry, chocolate, vanilla, cinnamon, or sugar glazing. They melted in your mouth. To this day, I can still taste the warm, sweet, fresh, homemade cake donuts. They were so good that people drove from miles around just to be there when Barnett's Dairyette opened at 6:00 a.m.

My friends were jealous because they assumed I could eat to my heart's content at the Dairyette for free. After all, I was Uncle Ervie's nephew. But that wasn't the case. In fact, my parents taught me at a very young age to never expect anything for free. By the age of four, my siblings and I were working in our big garden and picking wild blackberries for cobblers and jellies. By age seven, I was trying to find ways to earn a little extra money. My dad taught us how to pick poke greens and collect walnuts to sell at a local market. We also picked apples and peaches in my grandparents' orchard. By age eleven, I was old enough to get jobs working for other people. Many days, I would ride my bike by the Dairyette to see if Uncle Ervie had any work for me. One of my first jobs there was picking up trash in the parking lot. My payment? Fresh donuts and cold milk or a cheeseburger, fries, and a milkshake. I couldn't have been a happier young man.

In those days, when customers finished eating in their cars, they'd often toss their trash right out the window. Multiple times during the day the parking lot would be littered with empty paper cups, french fry trays, hamburger wraps, and corn dog sticks. My job was to pick up all the trash and then hose the parking lot down. And it didn't matter how long it took. Sometimes it would take an hour or more, and just when I thought I had it all clean, another french fry tray would fly from a car window and hit the asphalt, and I would start the process all over again.

If there was no trash to pick up, then Ervie would give me the job of hand-slicing fresh potatoes for the french fries. There was always plenty of work, and it was always worth it, especially since my compensation was delicious food that I couldn't get anywhere else. Sitting inside the Dairyette, dipping my warm donut into the ice-cold milk, I felt like I had really made it in life. I'd worked hard, the parking lot was clean, and all was right and good in the world.

I learned so much from Uncle Ervie. He was a hard worker and a very kind man, but it was his joy and generosity that really impacted me. Instead of just giving his nephews and nieces donuts, he consistently came up with work for us to do so we could experience the reward of honest work. He didn't have to do that. In

> *It was his joy and generosity that really impacted me.*

fact, Uncle Ervie was faced with several challenging life circumstances, growing up poor and having to go to work at age eight to help his family survive. Yet, he chose to open a restaurant, get up before the sun every day, go to bed after every street was empty late at night, and do the work—the work that God had called him to do. We all have struggles, and yes, unfair things happen to good people, but God has work for each of us to do. God had work for Uncle Ervie—which included owning the Dairyette—but in my life and in the lives of my siblings, his role was so much more than being a drive-in owner; his work included instilling a spirit of joy and generosity in us that would last forever.

ORDINARY CAN BE EXTRAORDINARY

Uncle Ervie had a third-grade education, and he was what most would call a "regular guy." He didn't come with any bells or whistles or big job titles. And yet, he made a huge difference in so many lives. Looking back on it, I see an ordinary man doing extraordinary things. He paid attention to me, he let me work alongside him, and he joyfully rewarded me with the best Barnett's Dairyette had to offer. God used Uncle Ervie in extraordinary ways, and He's working through you too. It's true! You really don't need money, three college degrees, the biggest house, and the nicest car to be extraordinary. You just need to give God your next steps—and then follow Him. He will take it from there.

LOOK AGAIN

QUESTIONS TO PONDER

Name a person from your past who poured into you—maybe someone who was considered ordinary. How did that person shape your life? How are you passing on what you learned to others?

CHAPTER 2

THE VIEW FROM THE BACK OF DAD'S OLD BUICK

PLANTING SEEDS

God is always planting seeds in us. And while we rarely realize what's going on at the time, we can look back and clearly see that things didn't just happen by chance. When I was four, Dad cooked up a plan. He wanted to take a big family vacation. As a pastor, he also wanted to attend a Christian convention in San Francisco. If he was going all that way, he figured he'd take the whole family, make a big deal out of it, and be gone for three weeks.

This plan to escape into the wide world seemed amazing to me. Could we do that? All of us just get in the car and leave? If Dad and Mom said so, it must be true, but my four-year-old mind just couldn't believe it. Were we really leaving Siloam Springs?

Dad drove a green and pink Buick, a hilarious-looking car with who knows how many miles on it. We thought this car was amazing because it had air conditioning. This thing was a tank. It was so wide you could sit four across the front seat comfortably. On a hot day in June, all nine of us piled in and hit the road.

That Buick had a big back window. I could crawl back there and fit just fine. In order to fit nine people in the car, four sat in the front seat, four sat in the back, and one of the smallest had to be on the floorboard or in the window. As the three youngest, Mark, Jonathan, and I took turns lying in the window or on the floorboard. One time I was tucked in the back window, and my mom noticed my arm in an odd position. She said, "James, watch out. Your arm is going to go to sleep from you lying on it that way." I said, "How? It doesn't have eyes." My siblings laughed and my mom and dad laughed. When you're the youngest in a big family, getting a laugh makes you stand tall. Mom repeatedly told that story from that day on. You know what? I didn't care if my arm fell asleep. I could see the whole wide world from that back window.

> *I could see the whole wide world from that back window.*

As we left Arkansas and headed across Oklahoma, I remember the excitement. It was my first time to take a road trip, my first time to leave what I knew as normal and explore new things. Looking out that back window, the world kept getting bigger and bigger. My horizons expanded with every mile.

This trip was no accident. God was igniting in me a passion for adventure, a belief in the power of prayer, a heart for exploring His creation, and a mind open to so many new possibilities.

A DESERT PRAYER

People have asked me why I believe in the power of prayer. They ask me how I know, without a doubt, that God is listening. Well, it all started when I was four years old, deserted on the side of the road in a very hot, dry, distant land with nothing but sand for miles and miles (so we thought).

You see, the Buick's air conditioner worked fine—when it didn't overheat. After we had been driving awhile, it would sometimes quit. So, when the radiator got hot, Dad stopped the car to rest. We'd all get out and stretch our legs for a bit, and then a few minutes later, we'd be on our way again.

It got hot that summer, especially in the middle of New Mexico and Arizona. We had stopped at Carlsbad Caverns, White Sands, and the Petrified Forest, and we were on our way to the Grand Canyon. We were driving through the night to get to the Grand Canyon for the early morning sunrise. In the middle of the night, our Buick overheated again, and we were stuck. You have to remember, this was 1962—no cell phones, no GPS, no internet. Most of the roads had only two lanes, and the population was sparse out there.

The night seemed eerily quiet. All around us was desert. No other cars or houses were in sight. We all got out of the car and stood on the side of the road. We looked both ways and waited for someone to come, but no one came. My dad started to pray. This wasn't new for us—he was a pastor, so we'd heard him pray lots of times. But now he sounded worried, anguished, even. I don't know exactly what that prayer was, but I know that he was desperate with his family in the middle of the desert. All of a sudden, he looked off into the desert and saw the moonlight reflecting on something. He took off walking toward it and discovered a small pond. He got some of that water, carried it back, and poured it into the Buick's old radiator. That did it. The car started right back up, and we were on our way again.

So, here's the truth. Maybe at the age of four I didn't exactly understand what was going on. But I did know that the car wasn't working, we were stranded on the side of the road in the middle of the night with no help in sight, my dad prayed, and then the car started! After he prayed, we were able to drive away to our next adventure. Does that mean that God always answers prayers for families with car trouble? No. He doesn't always answer prayers the way we think He should, but He did this time. I wonder why. Could it be that He was planting a seed in me? Today, I absolutely believe in the power of prayer, and the memory of my dad praying on the side of the desert road is ingrained in my mind. I can close my eyes and see it as clear as day. So, you tell me—accident, coincidence, or God at work?

TASTE OF NATURAL MAJESTY

Sometimes God's creation alone can embolden you to want to do great things. He created the most beautiful scenes for us to enjoy—snowy mountaintops, ocean waves, flowing waterfalls. How can we take in these unbelievable sights and not be inspired to do His work?

When we pulled up to the Grand Canyon, a thrilling rush flowed through me, and my horizons were expanded yet again. My dad was as excited as we kids were. This was his first time to see this wide-open canyon too! The vast chasm was unlike anything we had ever seen. My brothers and I got as close to the edge as we dared. The great, rushing river was a mile below, but what a view! I imagined a strong gust of wind could thrust me over the edge, causing me to fall for days, maybe. I wanted to go on the rim trail. My brothers did, too, so we took off. It was exhilarating, rushing headlong across the dusty canyon trails, hedged in by spruce and fir trees. I'd never seen anything so big in my life. It was one of those indescribable moments when you see how big God is and how small you are!

Before long, Dad called us back to the Buick. I wasn't ready for the experience to be over. I needed more time to drink it all in. I needed more time to grasp the magnificence of it all. I mean, my four-year-old mind was absolutely blown. I felt braver just by being in the presence of this huge, colorful, awesome masterpiece. I wanted to see more and more because I couldn't grasp it all at the same time. This stop had sparked my love for adventure and my heart for His creation—something I still have to this day—and it set my feet on a path to know God more.

God knew this would ignite the spark He placed in me, and He had a big plan to use it in a big way. This wasn't just a seed planted; no, this was an explosion, an overload to my senses, a real it-could-have-only-been-God moment. And just think—what if Dad had decided not to take this trip? If we had stayed home, would I have known any better? No. I wouldn't have known. But I also wouldn't have grown, the spark wouldn't have been ignited, and the leaps of faith my parents took would have never been witnessed. Who would have thought all that could have come from one family trip? Maybe it's time to go to the Grand Canyon again. Who's with me?

MOTEL WITH A POOL

Throughout this trip, God continued to refine this spark in me. With every new stop, new possibilities were born. For example, just when I thought I couldn't possibly be more wowed, we found a motel *with a swimming pool!* We had been sleeping in the car (all eight of us, while Dad or my sister drove) so we could "make more progress." But that night, my dad decided to rent a single room in a drive-up motel. I can still see the sign in my mind: *Vacancy! Free pool!* It was late when we arrived, so my parents insisted we get a good night's sleep. They took the bed, and we kids slept on the floor. We got to swim in that pool the next morning, and we thought that was the coolest!

From there, we drove into the city to visit the San Diego Zoo. Then Disneyland. Can you believe it? All of us at Disneyland! Then San Francisco. We walked across the Golden Gate Bridge and saw Alcatraz. We saw the San Francisco Giants Candlestick Park and then went with Dad to the convention. He was excited to attend, but after all that we'd experienced in the last week, we kids thought it was boring. We couldn't wait to get on the road again!

After the conference, we traveled through the Redwoods and on to Portland to visit my dad's sister. From there, most of my family drove three hours to Seattle to see the World's Fair. My brother Jonathan and I had to stay behind with my aunt. We were sad to miss out. At age eight, Mark was the youngest of us who got to go. They said the World's Fair was enormous with more people in one place than they'd ever seen. Somehow in the excitement, they lost sight of Mark. Dad was frantic. Anything could happen to a boy in a place that big and so far from home. My mom kept her head though. She kept saying, "We're going to find him. I just know it." They looked and looked and couldn't find him. What seemed like an hour passed, and they still hadn't found him. Then around a corner came a couple, and they were holding Mark's hand. They discovered Mark crying and asked him what was wrong. He said he was lost from his family. My mom's faith never failed her; she always believed the best.

On the way home, we returned by way of Yellowstone National Park. I'll never forget seeing Old Faithful. Waiting and watching for it to erupt was difficult for a fidgety boy of just four years old. But I was determined not to miss it. "When is it going to happen?" I kept asking. The minutes ticked by like hours. At last, the geyser erupted, bursting from the earth in a stream over one hundred feet high. Where was it all coming from? Would it ever run out? I felt my heart beating loudly in my chest. What a thrill! What a world God created!

Needless to say, I wasn't ready to go back home to Arkansas. I had seen so many amazing things, and my mind was open to so many new opportunities—opportunities I didn't know existed before this trip. My mind was swirling with unbelievable views—motels with swimming pools, the teacups at Disneyland, the vastness of the Grand Canyon, the eruption of Old Faithful—and I was excited about life. My four-year-old self would have stayed on that trip forever. God was laying the groundwork in my life, and He was moving in amazing ways—ways I didn't see yet, but I felt them with my whole heart, and I wanted more.

ONCE YOU SEE GOD WORK, YOU NEVER UNSEE IT

God used this trip to start building a faith in me that I still rely on to this day. He opened my eyes, He ignited a spark, and He showed me how prayer works. He used this trip to start building a foundation for my life. He is always working, friends. He's working in your life too. Even if you don't feel it or see it, lean into Him. No matter what age you are or what season of life you're in, God is working through you. Don't miss it! Spend some time today in prayer. Ask Him to show you where He's working, then join Him. Trust me;

===== LOOK AGAIN =====

once you see God work in your life, you can't unsee Him. "For it is God who works in you to will and to act in order to fulfill His good purpose" (Philippians 2:13 NIV).

QUESTIONS TO PONDER

When was the last time God sparked something in you? You don't have to go on a road trip across the country to see His work. Wherever you are today, look around. Now look again. Then close your eyes and thank God for all of it. How does pausing and appreciating God's work change your perspective?

CHAPTER 3

A POP-UP CAMPER IN THE BIG APPLE

GAME CHANGER

Seven years later, things had changed a bit. I was growing up, and I was finding that I really enjoyed being involved in the journey. I was no longer looking out the back window of the Buick; in fact, I had moved up to the front passenger seat (actually the middle front seat!). That's right! At the ripe age of eleven, I had been promoted, and success had never felt so good.

This trip came about because my brother Robert needed a way home. He was working at what we called a "rich kids' camp" in Vermont during the summer after his senior year of college. Dad hatched a plan—another big adventure! We would head northeast to pick up Robert. On the way he'd take us to visit all these great places: the Great Smoky Mountains; Washington, DC; Philadelphia; and New York City. By then there were three boys living at home: me (11), Jonathan (14), and Mark (15), and we were all game for Dad's plan. My grandmother, at age seventy-four, had only traveled outside Arkansas a few times before. Her husband had just passed away a few years earlier, so she was excited to join our family to see some new places. With Mom, that made us a party of six.

This trip was a game changer for me—not only because I had become fascinated with maps and figuring out the logistics of it all, but also because Dad invited me to help him plan our route. Weeks before the trip, he and I spent countless hours looking over maps, discussing the best possible routes, and thinking through each stop along the way. We planned for every turn and every exit, we prepared for busy intersections and heavy traffic areas, and we made sure there were plenty of places to pull over and sleep or stop for a picnic. I had it all lined out perfectly. Throughout the trip, Dad called me his "navigator." He'd say, "Where to, navigator?" I'd unfold the big map and watch for the signs. I'd say, "Okay, Dad, take a right up here onto this highway."

God works in mysterious ways. At the time, I thought

this was just a fun family trip, and I was excited to get in on the action. But now I know that He was igniting another spark He had placed in me—the spark to lead. My role as navigator was my first leadership position, and I took it seriously. Not only did I love leading, but I really enjoyed leading the ones I loved—my family. I wanted to find sleeping places near water because I knew my siblings loved to swim; I chose routes that would get us as close to the landmarks as possible because I knew my grandmother had a hard time seeing far away. And the look in their eyes when my plans worked—the ah-ha, this-is-out-of-this-world moments they experienced—well, I was a small part of making that happen for them, which only made me want to do more. To this day, leadership, to me, is an act of love. I want to be a part of a team, to help the team win, and I want us all to get to the ah-ha moments together. Through this trip, God ignited a spark in me that still lives on today. He works in mysterious ways, and He's always working. Do you see Him?

CAMPER IN TOW

Our Buick had long since been traded for a big Dodge

Coronado—another tank! And we had a new eyesore for this trip: a pop-up camper. It wasn't anything fancy, just the basic, pull-behind camper. At night, Dad figured we'd park somewhere, raise the roof of the camper, and slide out the beds. No air conditioning, no refrigerator, no frills whatsoever—just a place to sleep. We could stop anywhere we wanted for the night, and as the navigator, I had marked several places along our path to do just that.

We pulled that camper all the way from Siloam Springs through Tennessee, stopping in Nashville and Knoxville, then Gatlinburg, on through the Great Smoky Mountains National Park, up through Virginia. We drove into Washington, DC (I was exhilarated with the six lanes of traffic), saw the Washington Monument and the Capitol Building in the distance, walked by the Jefferson and Lincoln monuments, White House, Smithsonian Museum of Natural History, and then the Smithsonian National Air and Space Museum. And the fun didn't stop there! We drove to Philadelphia, taking in all the historical sites, including Independence Hall and the Liberty Bell. When I say we were in awe, I mean it was sensory overload. We were standing at monuments that we'd only ever read about. I felt like I could take over the world. If I could make it this far, ladies and gentlemen, I could do anything, or so I thought!

Next, we drove across the famous, massive George Washington Bridge into the largest city in the United States, New York City. It was like nothing we had ever seen—loud and fast and bustling. So much concrete and pavement, hundreds of big, tall

> *I felt like I could take over the world. If I could make it this far I could do anything, or so I thought!*

buildings, and so little green. We looked around some but had to keep moving because we were on a schedule. The camp in Vermont was closing up for the summer, and we needed to pick up Robert. Since our time was short, we began to make our way out of the city only to get lost and eventually end up in the Bronx. That's right, we hauled that old pop-up trailer up and down the streets of the Bronx. Can you imagine? A Dodge Coronado filled with six Arkansans pulling an eyesore of a camper up and down the streets for about thirty minutes until we found our way again. We must have been a sight!

Honestly, though, I don't know who got the bigger kick out of us—the people in the Bronx or the kids at the camp where Robert was working. We didn't think anything of it, of course, but we pulled that camper into the camp parking lot and set it up for the night. The next morning when parents arrived to pick up their children, well, there we were in all our glory. The best part of the deal was that Robert had to clean the cabins before he could leave. So naturally, my family jumped right in to help him finish. Once we all started cleaning, we began to find nickels, dimes, and other things the campers had left behind. We were even more excited to help after we made one new discovery after another! It was a good return as far as we were concerned, and we finished cleaning up in record time.

SHAKING HANDS WITH THE PRESIDENT

When I was sixteen years old, I took an interest in American government in high school. That summer, I was told there was a group of forty kids from Little Rock headed to Washington, DC, in a few weeks, and if I could find a way to the bus, I could go with them. I immediately said yes and then frantically went searching for someone to drive me the four hours to Little Rock. This was the first time I experienced a big trip without my family. Some of the kids complained, but not me. This bus was roomier than our old

Buick or Dodge or the pop-up camper, so in my opinion, it was pretty great.

In DC, we spent a full week learning about the political process and even did a Q&A event with Arkansas congressman John Paul Hammerschmidt. Meeting face-to-face with people working in the United States government was amazing to me. The highlight of the trip was a reception on the lawn behind the White House where around three hundred of us stood in line to shake President Nixon's and Vice President Ford's hands and have our pictures taken with them.

I couldn't believe it! Only a few years earlier I had been picking up trash for donuts and milk, and now I'm shaking the hands of the president and vice president! How does this happen? I determined then and there that there were no limits to what I could accomplish.

IGNITE THE SPARK
THAT GOD HAS PLACED IN YOU

When I got home from this trip, the spark God put in me had been fanned into a raging fire. I was confident and ready to kick my life into high gear. I started a Bible study at my house and excelled in multiple sports. I was confident in my relationship with God; I was saved, so no worries there. I was a driven achiever, and I was going to win. I was developing leadership skills, learning to be courageous, thinking outside the box, and effectively leading teams. However, when I "look again," I realize I was living in the "unconscious competent" zone, meaning I was unaware of why I was learning new skills and didn't know why I was succeeding in life. I mostly talked to God when I

LOOK AGAIN

wanted something from Him. I was doing my own thing and was grateful He was along for the ride. Can you relate? If God started a spark in you, and you took off without Him, it's not too late to turn around and invite Him to take the wheel. He is always there ready to take you on an exciting adventure!

QUESTIONS TO PONDER

What are some passions that God sparked in you at a young age? Have you ever lived in the "unconscious competent" zone? You know, when things are going smoothly and life seems to be on track, but you don't know why, and it still feels like something is missing?

PART TWO

DRIVEN OR CALLED?

CHAPTER 4

GOOD INTENTIONS

SOMETHING IS MISSING

Have you ever really thought about why you do the things you do? Why you're working at your job? Why you're coaching little league? Why you're volunteering at church? And furthermore, is *why* even the question to ask? You may think that your schedule is so packed that you aren't really choosing your daily activities but that they're choosing you. Does it feel like you're just going through the motions? It's easy to drift into that place. And the scary part is, it's just as easy to stay there if you're not paying attention.

That's where I was as a young adult. I was running full speed to do the "next thing" and get on with life. While I was a good athlete and had opportunities to play in college, sports weren't as important to me as getting my college degree, getting a job, and building something big—as quickly as possible. While I had some great opportunities with some big companies right out of college, I decided by this time that I liked starting small, building something, and watching it grow. As an entrepreneur, I was always buying and selling stuff to make a little money. Running a successful business was thrilling to me.

During my MBA program, I met two guys who owned a small business. They had just moved eight families from California to Arkansas to help grow their fledgling Christian greeting card company—Outreach Publications (now DaySpring). After visiting with them, I was intrigued. I asked them for a marketing intern job for the summer, and I loved every minute of it. Then I asked them for a full-time gig when I finished school a few months later. As a small company doing a little over one million dollars in sales with about thirty people, I was hoping they needed someone like me. And truthfully, I needed someone like them too. I was excited, and I launched into this job with gusto.

My adventurous spirit worked especially well for me in my career. Within a few months, I became the national sales manager and built a sales team of about thirty people over a few years. Soon after I started a marketing department and added eighteen more to the marketing team. I traveled a lot, spending about 125 nights on the road every year. The vision of DaySpring—to see every person experience and express the life-changing message of God's love—energized me. As a young company that focused on business and ministry, our primary customers were Christian bookstores at that time, but I had a bigger vision to expand into other markets and make our products available everywhere. It was a new thing for a Christian company like us to sell products in places like Walmart, gift stores, and grocery stores that had previously not carried inspirational products, and they weren't always receptive to the idea. It was a challenge— and I love a challenge!

In this role, I was able to meet new people, and I enjoyed developing new relationships. Hearing their stories and sharing our company's vision with them was energizing. Most of all, I enjoyed encouraging them to believe in themselves and serving them. Still, I felt pulled in two different directions—it was hard being away from my wife and young kids so much, but the company's mission resonated so much in my spirit too.

Like my dad and mom, I loved spending time with my family. So, when possible, my family would join me on summer business trips so we could see each other as much as possible. I made the effort to be involved in my kids' activities—I coached their sports, attended school events, and participated in family lake activities and get-togethers.

When I wasn't traveling, I was still working a lot. I'd go to the office when the kids left for school, then come home to have dinner. Once my wife, Marilyn, and I got the kids tucked in about 8:00 p.m., I'd go back to work until 2:00 a.m. How else could I get everything done? I had a growing sales and marketing team to run and accounts to manage. Besides, I reasoned, I didn't need much sleep. Five hours was fine by me. I had plenty of energy.

Looking back, I realize I was still working too much. I was an intense guy determined to achieve big things. I set goals and met them so I could achieve more goals. Still, something was missing.

THE BIG SHIFT

Are You Driven, or Are You Called?

The big shift came for me when I attended a leadership conference in 1988 where a man named Bob Buford told his story. This mega-successful businessman told us about his season of deep searching after his only child, a twenty-four-year-old young man, had died the previous year. That harrowing experience brought him to his knees. He struggled to understand why. Then something transformative happened: Buford was forced to choose between leaning entirely on God or just giving up. He saw how his life had been too focused on what he thought was important. He discovered a newfound intentionality.

His story shook me to the core. Like Buford, I'd been bulldozing my way through life. I was running toward a destination that seemed to be just over the horizon. I'd been checking things off my to-do list of success:

- Get my education. Check.
- Get married to a wonderful, beautiful woman. Check.
- Have kids. Check.
- Own a house. Check.
- Have a successful career. Check.

I began to ask myself the hard questions Buford raised: "Are you driven, or are you called? And do you understand the difference?"

Whoa. This was a shift. I didn't want to admit it, but all the evidence pointed to the fact that I was driven. Maybe I had good intentions, but not good results. In fact, my prayer life up to that point was pretty one-sided. I'd say, "God, I have this plan. Will You get on board and bless it, please?"

So, was I called, or was I just driven? I was saved by faith in Jesus Christ—I was convinced that I loved the Lord. I prayed often. I spent most of my waking hours working for DaySpring, a company on a mission to share God's love. I took my family to church every Sunday.

But was I "called according to His purpose" (Romans 8:28)? Did I listen for and discern God's voice, then follow Him? How might my life look different if I did? These were the questions I began to wrestle with.

I began to dig in by searching Scripture, praying, and seeking God's will. I also began seeking guidance from wise mentors. I read books by many great authors on these topics. I began to have a more earnest daily quiet time with the Lord, wanting to quit looking in the wrong places and learning to tune out the voices trying to distract me from hearing His voice. This was a big turning point for me.

God started to show me that I was asking the wrong question. The question isn't "How can I achieve *my* plan?" Instead, it's "What's *God's* plan, and how can I join Him in His plan?" I wanted to get in alignment with what God was doing. Whatever that was, it had to be better than my plan.

This was a major pivot point in my life, ushering me into a new season of discovery. Externally, I didn't immediately really make any radical life changes. But internally, I began paying more attention; I wanted to discover what *God* was up to rather than trying to lead Him to do what *I* wanted. Instead of trying to work *my* plan, I began to seek and implement *His* plan. I didn't do it perfectly, but I stayed with it, struggling to learn how to hear God's voice and follow His lead.

> *Instead of trying to work my plan, I began to seek and implement His plan.*

WHERE TO, GOD?

Marilyn and I talked about it, and like me, she wanted to be in alignment with God's plan. We knew it would take both of us working together. We both realized I was working too much, and together we would have to reprioritize things and stop letting my job drive so many of our decisions.

The good news is, I have a determined, strong, and committed wife. I saw those characteristics in her when we met in college. She is a woman of faith and gifted with many talents. Marilyn completed her elementary education degree in college and taught fifth grade for a few years until she turned her attention to raising our three children. She threw herself into volunteering at the school in the kids' classes, teaching Scripture to kids through the AWANA program at church, and using her talents as a wonderful vocalist, along with playing the flute and the piano. She was a leader on big family events and parties over the years, and if it had anything to do with our kids and investing in their lives, she was all in!

Over that year, I continued to follow our "new" plan. I wasn't really good at it, but I was determined. I began to do a lot of self-reflection. I thought about my upbringing and what my parents had taught me. They didn't have a lot, but they loved us generously, they gave us quality time, and they always involved us in their life activities. The experiences that kept coming to mind, though, were the family trips we took when I was four and eleven years old. I started thinking about how big an impact those trips had on me and my view of God. This is where I developed a passion for adventure and for experiencing God's magnificent creation. I wanted my kids to have that same experience and desire for discovery. An idea was born: Why not start taking two-week family vacations to experience God's creation through our national parks?

Up until then, we'd taken our young family on some short trips to experience the beauty of Arkansas and a few other places. But the decision to be intentional and take a couple of weeks every year to travel across the United States and take in God's creation by visiting as many national parks as possible, well, that was considered by many at that time to be a wild idea—but it's exactly what we did.

ARE YOU DRIVEN OR CALLED?

When I was asked to attend the leadership conference with hundreds of other up-and-comers in the business world, I thought I was really something. I was ready to make some connections, learn new business trends, and talk about how we were going to take over the world. But when I got there, it felt like Buford hit me over the head with a baseball bat. My eyes were opened to a whole new perspective. I learned that I was focusing on what I thought was good for me, and I was completely missing all the wonderful things God had planned. I discovered that I was asking all the wrong questions. Like me, maybe it's time for you to ask, "What's God's best?" and "What's His plan?" It might be time for your perspective and goals to

LOOK AGAIN

change too—to go from *your good* to *His best*. Trust me, when you decide to join Him in His work, your life will change in amazing ways—ways you never thought possible.

QUESTIONS TO PONDER

It's time to take a hard look at your life. Are you driven, or are you called? How can you begin asking yourself the right questions? What practical steps can you take to join God in *His* plan instead of asking Him to bless *your* plans? Ask God to give you new eyes to see life from His perspective.

CHAPTER 5

THE MAIDEN VOYAGE OUT WEST

THE PLAN

Ever thought you had a foolproof plan only to find out you didn't think everything through? Yeah, our first family trip was full of high expectations followed by some hard lessons. I was leaning into the plan God had for me, which I strongly believed included spending more quality time with my family and less time focused on work. But I learned that even when I tried following God's best plan, it didn't mean that everything was going to happen without a hitch.

Everyone knows the first step in planning for a trip is to pick the destination. To narrow it down, we decided to start with places within the United States that have "National Park" as part of their name, like Yellowstone National Park.

My sister Mary and her husband, Randy, and their two kids (ages fourteen and nine at the time) had similar ideas, so we excitedly put our heads together. Randy had a big passion for travel and seeing the national parks with his family, too, so we decided to do several trips with them. This worked out perfectly since our kids (ages seven, six, and one) enjoyed being with their cousins, and we loved being with Mary and Randy.

We went into "navigator" mode, spreading out maps on the kitchen table and making checklists of all the national parks. We studied the guidebooks, atlases, and all the literature we could find. Then it was time to go! We launched into the adventure at full throttle. We took two cars this first trip—my sister, brother-in-law, and their family in one, and ours in another.

AWAY WE GO

Our first stop was in Dillon, Colorado, a great place for families. It was pure joy exposing our kids to new places and getting to see their faces light up as they experienced things for the first time. One of our first experiences together as a family was riding down an alpine slide, a bobsled-like ride down the side of a ski mountain. The 2,500-foot slide drops more than 600 vertical feet at twenty to thirty miles per hour. It was a breathtaking experience.

So far, our plan was working. We were a happy family on an amazing adventure, our kids were famously getting along

> *It was pure joy exposing our kids to new places and getting to see their faces light up as they experienced things for the first time.*

with their cousins, and this wild trip idea was everything we were missing. But our next stop, Arches National Park in Moab, Utah, would give us a new perspective on traveling, especially with kids.

EXPECTATIONS AND GOD'S PLANS

We'd driven a long way that day, and with the recurring question "Are we there yet?" coming from the back seat every five to ten minutes, I could tell that the kids were tired of being in the car. And honestly, I was tired of them being in the car too. I wanted to let them out, but unfortunately, the hard truth was, we weren't "there" yet.

When we finally arrived, the kids were so full of energy, they excitedly jumped out of the vehicles, ready to experience everything the Arches National Park had to offer.

I just knew this experience would be amazing—the kids were definitely going to love it. I mean, the park is a natural wonderland of geological marvels, with varying hues of red sandstone and over two thousand natural stone arches rising high into the air. It was time for a hike—time for the family to "take it in" and "mark the moment." We started on a hike to Delicate Arch. It's a fifty-two-foot-tall freestanding natural arch and widely recognized landmark—one of the most beautiful sights I've ever seen. To see Delicate Arch up close, though, you have to hike a couple of miles and climb up approximately five hundred feet. *No problem*, I thought. *We've been cooped up all day saving our energy for this. Let's do this!* So off we went.

Our kids had no fear. They were running across the tops of gigantic ridges, and we were letting them; we were glad they were getting some of that pent-up energy out. But then we got closer and saw that on the other side of the ridges was a fifty-foot drop. Terrified for their safety, we immediately grabbed them off the ridges and made sure they knew running on those ridges was no longer an option.

We got about halfway to Delicate Arch before the kids' excitement began to dwindle, and they just couldn't take another step. They were hot and tired and hungry. In fact, Marilyn and I had to carry them on our backs halfway up the trail and halfway down it. With every step, I was pointing out the beautiful landscapes and vistas, God's amazing creation surrounding us. I was in awe of His beautiful handiwork, and I just knew that if the kids could see it, they would be amazed too. They were impressed, just not quite as much as I was.

By the end of the hike, though, I had realized a couple of things: one, the kids didn't always see things the way I did; and two, they didn't care very much about the beauty of creation at that moment because they were hungry needed to get them some food—fast!

We hurriedly drove back into town for dinner. We went to the first restaurant we saw—Pizza Hut. We were all starving, and as soon as we walked in, I asked, what can we order that will arrive the fastest?" They said, "We got some spaghetti made." So, we asked them to bring spaghetti right away. They brought it out soon as we sat down. I've never seen kids eat so fast. Nobody said a word—we all tucked in and ate our spaghetti in a flash. We ordered pizza too—we were so hungry from all that hiking. Needless to say, that night we all slept well.

Over ten days or so, we visited, toured, and hiked many miles in Canyonlands, Natural Bridges, Monument Valley, Four Corners, and Mesa Verde, and we experienced multiple other adventures as well. We rode the Durango and Silverton train through the iconic Horseshoe Curve, and High Bridge, and along the Animas River Gorge. Wow! What an experience! With each new place came new experiences and new firsts.

Soon it was time to head back to Arkansas. On the way home, we stopped in Santa Fe, New Mexico, for one last hoorah and toured the Old Town and the capitol building. A highlight of our last major stop was having ice cream and a picnic in the Plaza to celebrate our wonderful, inaugural trip to kick off our national park extravaganza. What an amazing journey!

EXPECTATIONS VERSUS REALITY

I learned two key lessons during this inaugural trip. Lesson one: dreaming of what the future holds is okay unless it slides into expectation mode. I had a vision in my head of how hiking the Arches was going to go: my kids were going to light up in wonder at the breathtaking views as they walked alongside Marilyn and me. But reality and expectations rarely align. I'm only disappointed when my expectations collide with reality. Lesson two: not everyone is going to see it the same way. I could have walked for miles in amazement at the wonders that surrounded me, but my kids at the time—not so much. If I were to do it again, I would go a little slower. I would have watched a little closer to see what God was doing and guided my kids to His best. If you're like me, you, too, have been disappointed when plans didn't quite go as expected. But it's during those times that God reminds us to slow down, take a breath, and trust His plan (Proverbs 19:21).

QUESTIONS TO PONDER

When was a time that your expectations didn't match your reality? How loosely do you hold your expectations, whether for a big trip or for what's happening tonight or tomorrow morning? How can you adjust your own expectations to the expectancy of what God is doing and avoid disappointment in the future?

CHAPTER 6

BADLANDS, BEARS, AND BISON

RIDING IT OUT

Life isn't always an exciting adventure. There are times when you'll be on top of the mountain seeing the most beautiful sights and praising God for His amazing ways, and there are other times when you'll find yourself in the lowest part of the valley surrounded by heavy darkness that won't let even a sliver of light in. But the highest of highs and the lowest of lows don't make up the majority of your time. No, most days are just regular days. Most days are spent living "in the meantime" on what I call the side of the mountain—not on the top or on the bottom, but somewhere in the middle.

Living "in the meantime" is harder than one might

think. It requires plodding along and waiting on next steps, maintaining hope that something good is going to happen someday, and overcoming minor setbacks that can weigh you down. This next trip forced my family and me to slow down, find the beauty in everyday occurrences, and pay attention to one another. And while slowing down isn't really in my nature, I have to say, the discipline of stopping to "smell the roses" has granted me a much wider view of who God is and how He works.

With a trip out West under our belts, our family was ready to venture a little farther north into the wild. We set out for the Badlands National Park in South Dakota. With my sister and her family, we piled into a big fifteen-passenger van and hit the road.

There's a rhythm to road-tripping. An exciting sense of anticipation is the baseline. That baseline hums along, even as you traverse mile after mile of unchanging road. And then that excited expectation gradually turns into something like a gnawing hunger. Traveling with multiple families requires that you lean into those humdrum feelings. You learn to ride them out in faith that something good is on the other side of that present, sometimes unpleasant, feeling.

And isn't that the same in life? Sometimes living "in

the meantime" is following a daily routine, and that can easily start to feel like we're stuck in a car for hours on end. Nothing is changing. We feel like we're never going to get to our destination, and it's so easy to give up hope that there is anything good at the end of this. Ultimately, we just get tired of waiting. Friend, I've been here. I'm *really* not good at waiting, and I don't like to sit still. But I've found during these times that if I keep looking for where God is working, I can see Him work in a different way.

Are you in this season? Do you feel as if you're just waiting for something—and while you have no idea what it is you're waiting on—you know that where you are today is not forever? If so, please know this: He's still working in the people around you, the town He's placed you in, and your day-to-day tasks. It may not feel like it, but He's got good plans lined up for you. He's working out His plans for your life, but you may need to wait for Him to move the pieces around and get you exactly where He needs you to be. Or He may be preparing your heart for your next steps—only He knows. But if you don't slow down long enough to look for it, you'll miss seeing His plan at work (Psalm 46:10). So, what I've found (and I still struggle with this) is if I keep leaning into God and believing His plans are good (Romans 8:28),

I'll come through the "in the meantime" days and end up stronger and wiser and closer in my relationship with Him. This isn't easy, but it's good.

WHAT HAPPENS IN THE MEANTIME

There was a lot of "on the way" and "in the meantime" on this trip. With the first day being a twelve-hour drive, there was a lot of car time to try to entertain the kids. But we were off very early, and we were excited!

The first park we planned to visit on this trip was Badlands National Park in South Dakota. We needed a place to stay the first night, so we chose a cheap motel in the town of Wall. Driving into South Dakota, we couldn't help but see the signs to a place called Wall Drug. First it was "Free ice water at Wall Drug!"; then a few miles later, "Homemade Ice Cream at Wall Drug!" By the time we got near Wall, the family was so pumped about this drug store that we had to stop at this roadside attraction.

We walked into Wall Drug, prepared for something spectacular after all that hoopla. And while I thought the place really wasn't much to look at, we found out that it had become a major tourist attraction, visited by more than two million people each year. It sells local goods and just about every souvenir you can dream of—T-shirts, bumper stickers, snow globes, silver spoons, pot holders, salt and pepper shakers—all to mark the occasion of visiting their rather unusual store. It even included a huge restaurant. The kids loved the statue of the giant jackalope (part jack rabbit, part antelope). Since there was nothing for another fifty miles in either direction, it became an unexpected destination on our journey.

While the rest of the family looked around the store and delighted in all the little trinkets, I was trying to slow my mind down and start "enjoying" our vacation. Coming out of a few busy weeks of work and all the pressures of life, I was still going a hundred miles an hour in my mind. It was then that I realized I was doing it again. I was rushing, rushing, rushing, and I was missing it all. When I looked around the store, I saw my kids, along with my nieces, Ashley and Allison, running around and smiling, showing each other the little treasures they found; they were really enjoying one another and the moment.

And I was missing it! I made a decision right there in Wall Drug: I wasn't going to rush through this trip, because when I was going eighty miles an hour trying to get to the top of the mountain, I missed the thrill of seeing my family experience something for the first time. And I never wanted to miss that again! I wanted to watch their eyes and their expressions; I wanted to watch their faces light up in awe. I had missed all of that because I was too focused on going, going, going. I find that when I slow down, I can see God working. And even better, I get to see how He's working through the people around me. I didn't want to miss that! I had to slow down, refocus, and engage in the moment.

Once my perspective changed, I started to relax. *Don't hurry,* I told myself, *let the kids have fun. After all, they've been in the van for twelve hours!*

Early the next morning, we arrived at Badlands National Park, with hundreds of miles of rugged beauty. Its wide-open prairies and seemingly endless expanses of rock mountains stole my breath away; the sharply eroded buttes and pinnacles were spectacular. The hue of rock and sand layers were colorful and vivid. We spent the day driving around the scenic byway loop, taking time for some hiking along the way. I thought of the thousands of years of wind and weather that forged such odd-shaped tiers, ridges, and spires. Just like the wind and weather, God was using the experiences on this trip to shape me too.

VISION CASTING

Mount Rushmore astounded on a different level. Having seen pictures of the memorial of America's founding fathers, George Washington, Thomas Jefferson, Theodore Roosevelt, and Abraham Lincoln, I still wasn't prepared to take in the size of it. It's enormous. The sculptures carved into the side of a mountain are over sixty feet tall—the size of a six-story building! Just the nostril of one of these presidents is the size of a grown man! We talked about why this memorial had been made and how different life would be if these great leaders hadn't lived.

What blew me away at Mount Rushmore was imagining the planning, the strength, and the vision it took to accomplish the feat of creating this monument. I couldn't wrap my head around the patience it must have taken to create this massive masterpiece.

Now, stay with me here. God was teaching me about patience and rest, right? I was learning about slowing down so I could see what He was up to. He was teaching me about how to live "in the meantime." And it just so happens that one of the destinations on this trip was a national memorial that took fourteen years to construct. A few hundred workers, most of whom were miners, sculptors, or rock climbers, showed up every day for fourteen years straight and literally chiseled away on the side of a mountain until Mount Rushmore became what it is today: a national treasure. My family was taking it in. I was taking it all in. God had my attention.

BISON CROSSING

Though the national parks were the main goal of the trip (or so we thought), we wanted to visit the state parks and other points of interest when we could. Custer State Park, located in the southwest corner of South Dakota, is enormous at over 71,000 acres. It's a very curvy drive to get there. The first fourteen miles along the way to the park is called Needles Highway. It's a constant series of curves and switchbacks where you can drive only twenty to thirty miles per hour. You drive up, through, and around mountains; then the road flattens out a little, and you look up and see these beautiful standing mountains with rock formations.

Driving along the winding roads, we came to a place where the bison roam free, just as they had for centuries before. Though they had almost been extinct at one time, they'd come back, and now here they were—hundreds and hundreds of them! These beautiful creatures gave no thought to the cars or people. Why would they, at their size? They wandered right over the road, oblivious to the signs, the people, or the cars. That's right, you guessed it. Hundreds of bison had wandered right into the road, and they weren't budging. I thought, *This was not in the plan!* At that moment, all I could do was look up to God and say, "I hear You, Lord! Loud and clear. I'm slowing down, I'm taking my time, and I'm taking it all in."

And that's exactly what I did. I stopped the van, grabbed my camera, and walked right up close to the herd to capture the moment. Other travelers came along and stopped too. I cautioned the kids, "Be safe—don't get too close." These creatures were mesmerizing, their dark brown coats gleaming as the sun shone down. It was such a phenomenal moment. We were hushed and quiet, watching them in awe, as multiple camera shutters clicked. After what seemed like an hour, the whole lot of them had finally meandered across the road.

In the end, I was grateful they'd given us a reason to pause. To take it all in. To store the moment in our memories. I'd invested a lot of time pouring over maps and guidebooks, calculating hours and daylight—I didn't really like to let go of my plan. But the bison forced me to relax and accept a bigger plan. It was clear that God had better plans than mine, and if I had rushed it, I would have missed it altogether.

> *It was clear that God had better plans than mine, and if I had rushed it, I would have missed it altogether.*

After touring Custer State Park, we swung back north and drove the seventy-plus miles past numerous lakes and dense ponderosa pines to our next destination, a little town called Deadwood, South Dakota. It used to be a mining town where Wild Bill Hickok, Wyatt Earp, and Calamity Jane are rumored to have lived for a time. From there, our next stop was Devils Tower in northeast Wyoming, a butte rising 1,267 feet above the Belle Fourche River. Just amazing! We then traveled south across the wide-open high plains and expansive ranches of Wyoming and along the North Platte River, taking in the views. We were surprised by the immense beauty of the Big Thompson Canyon as we drove from Fort Collins to Estes Park, Colorado. While staying in Estes Park, we went on many wonderful and strenuous hikes. We saw bears, elk, deer, beautiful streams and falls, and mountain vistas along the way.

LEARN TO LIVE "IN THE MEANTIME"

Life isn't one awesome moment after another. Life is mostly made up of those "in the meantime" moments. Stopping at Wall Drug with the family, having a front-row seat at Mount Rushmore, and then literally being stopped by a herd of bison all slowed me down. It taught me to embrace the "in-between" moments and, instead of trying to run to the next thing, to look around for what God is doing right in that moment. After this trip, I made a decision that I would process the "disappointment" of setbacks and slow-downs in life a little differently. Instead of being frustrated that I'm not moving fast enough—whether that be a move up in my job or a slow car in front of me while I'm trying to get somewhere—I now force myself (and

I'm sure not perfect at it) to reset my mind and focus on God's plan (Philippians 4:4–9). When we slow down, we see Him in the people around us, notice the beauty and strength in His creation, feel the weight of the bison's steps, and see the wonder in my children's eyes. This is the good stuff. Let's not miss it.

QUESTIONS TO PONDER

How could slowing down change your perspective? How do you see God "in the meantime"—not when you're on the mountaintop or in the valley, but when you're on the side of the mountain? How can you better embrace the "in between" moments in everyday life?

PART THREE

FINDING THE EXTRAORDINARY IN THE ORDINARY

CHAPTER 7

NIAGARA FALLS: RAISING THE BAR

SEIZE THE DAY

As a young family man, I was doing my best. While I hadn't perfected it by any means, I was trying to listen to what God had for me next. I was intent on making sure my steps matched His calling and that I wasn't just out there making my own moves for my own reasons. I was trying to hold all my expectations loosely. I wanted God to know He could change my plans at any time for any reason. And I was learning to be okay with slowing down and looking for "wow moments" in everyday experiences. Then I ran across this verse: "I pray that the *eyes of your heart* may be enlightened in order that you may know the hope to which He has called you" (Ephesians 1:18 NIV; emphasis mine).

I paused. Something stopped me in my tracks. How

do you see with the *eyes of your heart*? This verse really intrigued me. The more I pondered, studied, and asked God about it, the more He started to show me. I started to see people, places, circumstances, things—*everything*—through the lens of God's understanding and love. I realized that unless God opened my eyes to His work, I couldn't see properly. Truthfully, I'm blind unless He opens my eyes (II Kings 6:15–18). This was another huge pivot point for me. I no longer wanted to go about my everyday business, doing my everyday tasks, with blinders on. I wanted to see the whole

> *of my heart, I wanted to celebrate every moment, every person, and every situation.*

view. When God opened the eyes of my heart, I wanted to celebrate every moment, every person, and every situation. I wanted to *seize each day*; I wanted to live it to the fullest!

When you're seeing through the lens of God's love as revealed by the Holy Spirit, you can't help but want to soak it all in—the amazing views, the beautiful people, the life circumstances, the hard times, the hope of tomorrow, and the restoration of all of it. I was learning that God was in and through every moment, and I wanted a front-row seat. In this season of my life, I started to find ways to seize the day or carpe diem (as they say). I wanted my new lens to lead me, and I wanted to share it with others.

DON'T MISS OPPORTUNITIES

I loved to travel for work and meet new people, but I often thought to myself, "I wish Marilyn and the kids were here." I was planning to attend an upcoming trade show in Ottawa, Canada, and I wanted my family to experience this new place with me. So, I planned a two-week family trip through Missouri, Illinois, Indiana, Ohio, Pennsylvania, and New York on our way to the convention. With my kids being ten, nine, and three, this was the perfect time and age for them to experience America and its beauty! They would learn how to seize the day and how to see God's awesomeness in everything. It was another time for them to start "taking it in," and I couldn't wait for them to be a part of it.

THRILL RIDES

Our first stop was in Ohio, a good twelve-hour drive from our home. We bought tickets to Cedar Point, an amusement park situated right on Lake Erie. Our thrill-seeking kids, along with their mom and their thrill-seeking dad, had a blast in this park. After all, they had the highest and fastest roller coasters in the world! After a few days we were off again.

We drove through the corner of Pennsylvania, making our way northeast toward the Finger Lakes area of New York. They're called Finger Lakes because they're eleven long and narrow bodies of water. The kids kept saying, "It's so green here!" There was an abundance of water: creeks, rivers, springs, lakes. It was such a contrast to the deserts of the West we'd visited the summers before.

After checking out all the lakes, we spent the night in Ithaca and made time to see beautiful, historic Cornell University and Ithaca College. Then it was off to the Thousand Islands area in upper New York, along the border of the United States and Canada. This area vastly exceeded my expectations. The vastness of the St. Lawrence River and the incredible sight of more than 1,800 islands in one area was truly inspiring. Incredible views, beautiful retreats, and a hub of outdoor activities filled our senses. We soon crossed over a massive bridge and started our final leg to Ottawa.

Throughout the trip, from the roller-coasters to the Finger Lakes to the Thousand Islands surrounded by boats, I continuously reminded my family to "take it in." And what I meant by that was *look deeper—do you see it?* There's so much more to things than what we see at first glance. Keep looking, and open the eyes of your heart—look for what God is showing you, and be ready to be amazed.

ACCEPTING REST

It seemed like we did a lot more sightseeing by car on this trip than we'd done on our previous trips—we did log a lot of driving hours. And it wasn't easy to "seize the day" when I was driving mile after mile through what looked like the same big city and the same small town over and over. I remember one stretch across New York when I was tired, and to tell you the truth, I felt a little uneasy about how quiet the car was. *Maybe I should start a game or see if I could lead the family in a sing-along,* I thought. I was racking my brain for what I could do in these dull moments to bring the excitement of adventure back in the vehicle, to ignite the spark again. And just when I was about to throw out an "I spy something...," I noticed it—the kids were either silent or asleep, and my wife looked perfectly content sitting next to me and looking out the window. After all, she could go for hours without speaking and be just fine (something I was not very good at). So, I just drove on and enjoyed the sights, embracing the silence and peace.

It made me realize that not everybody needs to be fully energized—running on cliffs, dodging bison, or screaming their heads off on roller-coasters—to live in the moment with God. In fact, embracing rest and relaxation is a big part of living in the moment. When we can be quiet with God and let the stillness and the serenity of His love wrap around us, there's no better place to be. In fact, we need this time to restore and renew us so we can see Him more clearly. So, despite my desire to get everyone involved in another activity, I decided to let them be. Let them rest. Let them sleep and let them enjoy it. After all, resting was part of seizing the moment—it was part of "taking it all in." As we drove along in silence, I smiled, so thankful for my family, for this moment with them, and for God's unfailing love.

THE BAR IS RAISED

When at last we arrived in Ottawa, the capital city of

Canada, my family was really impressed, and so was I. The city is situated right on the Ottawa River. It's beautiful. The first thing I noticed was how clean the city is. Even though a few million people live and work there, it didn't seem very busy. Water taxis took tourists and residents from place to place via the waterways. It was a new, fun experience for us to ride around in the water taxis. Something else new for us? Staying in something other than a camper or two-star motel! We stayed in a big, fancy hotel on a high floor overlooking the city. This hotel had bellhops, room service, and lush bathrobes hanging on hooks in the bathroom. The kids were over the moon, and I loved watching their faces light up with each new discovery. It was exactly how I felt when we found that motel with a swimming pool when I was four years old. It expanded their horizons, and with every road trip, their world just kept getting bigger and bigger. Their minds were being opened to new possibilities. And again, I would challenge them, saying, "There's more to this than a fancy building and some nice bathrobes! What's truly happening here? Remember, God is always working."

It would be a while before we stayed in a hotel that nice again. In fact, the next summer we went back to staying with friends and family along the way. But for five nights, the kids thought they had hit the mark, and Marilyn and I enjoyed it too. We got such a kick out of watching the kids' reactions to the impressive accommodations. During the day I had work meetings, so Marilyn and the kids spent the time roaming the city and enjoying the shopping and sights. Then we'd meet up later and catch up over dinner.

WONDER AND AWE

Next up was Niagara Falls State Park, the oldest state park in the United States, where we met up with our best friends, David and Amy Brooker. We were excited they were joining us for this part of the adventure.

We found a hotel close to the falls on the Canadian side and quickly walked down to explore and get a closer look at the massive falls. As we gazed down at the water coursing over the cliffs with astounding power and heard the roar of the falls, I remembered visiting here as a kid. The energy of it struck a chord somewhere deep inside me. I was reminded of Psalm 29:3–5 (NIV):

The voice of the LORD is over the waters; the God of glory thunders, the LORD thunders over the mighty waters. The voice of the LORD is powerful; the voice of the LORD *is majestic. The voice of the* LORD *breaks the cedars; the* LORD *breaks in pieces the cedars of Lebanon.*

I kept thinking, *God spoke this thing into existence!* His creativity and power were on full display. The intensity and noise made me feel speechless. This natural wonder is all for God's glory and God's pleasure. In His goodness, He shares all of creation with us. All we have to do is show up and keep our eyes open. And that is exactly what I intended to do.

We didn't know it then, but my best friend since childhood, David, age thirty-two at this time, would develop a brain tumor and pass away eighteen months later—which makes this trip even more meaningful as I look back on it. It really taught me the importance of making time for those who mean the most to you. What if I hadn't decided to seize the day, to make the most of this trip? I would have missed these moments with my best friend and regretted not doing more with him before it was too late. I'm so thankful that I can replay the memories in my mind of this last major trip together. But I'm getting ahead of myself.

FACING YOUR FEAR

On our way home we went through St. Louis so we could visit the Gateway Arch National Park. When you arrive in St. Louis, the Arch is the first thing you see. Standing at 630 feet, this thing is huge—even taller than the Washington Monument. It dominates the landscape, towering over the skyscrapers. It truly is a triumph of engineering.

I'll admit, I'm a little claustrophobic. I don't like tight spaces, and they don't like me. As a six-foot-three man, I don't fit well in small places. Even as a kid I remember going into some local caves near where I grew up, and I really never liked it. Yet, I was excited to go in the Arch—until I saw the elevator pod that took us to the top. It was tight! It was more uncomfortable for me than any roller-coaster ride at Cedar Point. I found myself sitting knee to knee with five other people in a tiny little space. I couldn't help but think, *What if this thing gets stuck?* I put on a brave face and went up to the top of the Arch. Of course, I knew that

> *Sometimes "seizing the day" means you have to do something even though it scares you a little.*

I'd have to get back into that tiny space to come back down, but I refused to let fear hold me back from the experience. And you know what? The view was amazing and so worth the short-lived discomfort. Sometimes "seizing the day" means you have to do something even though it scares you a little. It means you need to lean on God, pray for courage, and then trust Him.

SEIZE THE DAY!

Looking back on this trip, I see that God opened my eyes to view everything in a new light. I knew that I needed to rethink my busy work schedule. During this trip, I was able to watch my children's faces light up in awe of His majesty. I expanded their minds the way my dad had expanded mine. I learned how to *seize each moment*, even the quiet, uneventful ones. Best of all, I was able to spend time with my best friend, David, and his wife, Amy, at one of the most beautiful places on earth. God opened the eyes of my heart, and when I saw the views, people, and places through His lens, it changed everything. He's ready to open the eyes of your heart too. Are you ready for a new perspective?

LOOK AGAIN

Now, your perspective will be different than mine. Everyone seizes the day differently. For me, slowing down and smelling the roses is harder, and for someone else, speeding up is harder. There's good in both! Whatever you do, don't miss the chance to make big impacts out of ordinary, everyday moments. Don't miss the beauty that surrounds you and the everlasting love that's in and through it all. Look again!

QUESTIONS TO PONDER

As you reflect on your life, what are some things you've done that you're glad you did? What are some things you regret not doing? What held you back? What can you do differently to seize each moment and embrace the rest, the adventure, and everything in between?

CHAPTER 8

FLORIDA:
TOO CLOSE FOR COMFORT

IT'S ABOUT PEOPLE

Whenever we took a trip, we always tried to stop and see family and friends along the way. We sometimes even made new friends. From time to time, someone would invite us someplace new. Interestingly, some of those adventures resulted in the best trips of all.

Roger and Cheryl, our good friends from college, invited us to visit them in Florida. I had a convention to attend for work in Orlando, so I figured we could make a big trip of it (seize the day!), and maybe there would be some national parks along the way. Marilyn and the rest of the family could visit Disney World and other local attractions while I worked. So, we planned the trip!

GRAND PURSUITS

We spent a couple of days visiting Roger and Cheryl at their home in St. Augustine. After that, we headed down the east coast of Florida toward Cape Canaveral. It had only been a couple of years since the tragic Space Shuttle *Challenger* explosion in 1986, so I had a healthy respect for the risks these folks were undertaking. I wanted our kids to respect them, too, so we visited the Kennedy Space Center, where we learned all about America's pursuit of new frontiers in space. I was excited for them to learn about the original moon landing, which I'd watched live on television as a young child. I can still hear Neil Armstrong utter those famous words: "That's one small step for man, one giant leap for mankind."

We headed south to West Palm Beach to take in the sights, then west across Alligator Alley to the Everglades National Park, where over a million acres of wildlife quietly waited for exploration. Contrary to the loud crashing waves and business of the beaches, the Everglades offered unassuming wilderness waterways. We had a great time on the airboats zipping through twisting mangrove tunnels looking for alligators and pythons and other creatures.

What an adventure!

Next, we drove around Marco Island and Naples, where the water is emerald green and soft, white, sandy beaches beckoned. Then it was back up the west coast of Florida and on to Orlando, where I had a convention to attend, and Marilyn and the kids were anxious to get to Disney World.

TOO-FAST CARS

The most memorable part of our Florida road trip was the day Roger and Cheryl took us to one of the beaches on the Atlantic Ocean. I'd been to the Atlantic Coast before but nowhere like this. People treated those gorgeous stretches of sand like any other highway. It was normal to drive right up next to the water. So early one morning, we drove right up onto the beach and parked, along with four hundred other cars. Then we walked about three hundred yards and put our chairs and beach towels by the water. The waves were bigger there than we were used to on the gulf side of Florida, and I knew that could mean danger for unsuspecting kids, so I stayed busy keeping a close eye on them as they played in the waves near the water's edge.

By midday the beach was packed. Between us and our

parked car, a roadway had appeared, and cars were moving at thirty, forty, and even fifty miles an hour up and down it. Around lunchtime we headed back to the car to get some food. The older kids came with me and Roger, but little three-year-old Jordan stayed behind with Marilyn and Cheryl. But when Jordan turned and saw us walking toward the car, he suddenly took off running after us, leaving his mom behind. To this day, I don't know why Roger turned around, but he did. Out of the corner of his eye, he saw Jordan running toward us and all those speeding cars.

Roger yelled, "Jordan, stop!" I've never heard Roger yell that loudly in my life.

Jordan froze. I turned just in time to see his terrified face as a car whizzed by. He must have felt the swoosh of air as it sped past, barely missing him by less than a foot. Talk about a "wow" moment! In the space of that moment, my heart sank and then sang—I was terrified, then overjoyed. I ran back and scooped Jordan up. Immediately I began to pray, "Lord, thank You, thank You, thank You for sparing Jordan's life."

> *In the space of that moment, my heart sank and then sang—I was terrified, then overjoyed.*

I set him down, and like nothing serious had happened, he ran off to play in the ocean. For me, the rest of that day was a blur. I couldn't shake the image or feeling of Jordan's near miss.

Marilyn, Nick, and Abbey saw it too, and they were sobered as well. What a wake-up call. For the rest of the trip we were on high alert. We kept a closer eye on all the kids, but especially on Jordan.

THE FACADE OF CONTROL

Here I was, with a few successful trips under my belt, and *I thought I had it all under control.* Then while I wasn't paying attention, Jordan almost lost his life. I realized right then and there, no matter how much I tried as a parent, I was never in control. Ever. The truth is, we're always on a ledge, and God is watching over us. He holds on to all His children, and He doesn't let us go. He's so much bigger than anything we could ever imagine, and He's already planned things out. Here I was carrying around a *false sense of security.* I thought I trusted God, but really, I was only trusting Him with certain things. I realized that the real reason I was trying to control things is because I wanted them to go my way. "You can control it, Lord, as long as You do what's in my plan; however, if you deviate from what I think should happen, I'm going to need that control back, okay?" Unfortunately, that's just not how it works. He's in charge, and it's His plan. He's in control, not us.

If I'm being truthful, I still struggle with this. So, I just keep laying it down at His feet, and every time I do, He fills me with peace. He'll do it for you too. He's ready to take the worry, fear, pain, and shame away. Lean into Him. He really does have this. And trust me, striving to gain control of your life will wear you out—and it's not possible anyway. But that's okay, because God's got us.

QUESTIONS TO PONDER

Why do you try to hold on to control? Is it because you want your way? What would life be like if you released total control to God? How would it feel? Do you trust God with only certain things in your life or everything? How do you know?

CHAPTER 9

MAJESTIC MOUNTAINS

YIPPEE

Enthusiasm is contagious. I've found this to be true at home, work, sporting events—everywhere really! You see, I'm naturally an enthusiastic person. People say I bring energy into the room whether I try to or not. So every time I returned from a trip, I enjoyed telling all my friends and family about the unbelievable sights, the exciting adventures, and sometimes the scary moments. Well, the enthusiasm caught on, and word continued to get out among our friends and family about our road trip adventures. When folks learned how much fun we were having, they wanted to join us. That was fine by me—the more the merrier!

> Enthusiasm is contagious.

This particular year, we started out with our normal

party of nine, but that grew to twenty-two people along the way! Wow! If I was excited with *nine people*—having *twenty-two people* on the journey was a dream come true. I'm passionate about bringing people along on the journey, sharing experiences with them, and inspiring them to see all God has for them.

On this trip, it was my family of five, along with my parents, three of my siblings and their families, and our friend Amy. Because our destinations were Grand Teton National Park, Yellowstone, and Glacier National Park, they all wanted to come along. Our plan was for everyone to meet in Jackson Hole, Wyoming, and travel together from there.

At our first stop, Grand Teton National Park, we took a shuttle boat onto the pure waters of Jenny Lake, which is tucked into the base of the mountains of the Teton Range. Jenny Lake's water was calm, pristine, and deep blue. From the boat, we got a terrific view of Teewinot Mountain, Mount Saint John, and Cascade Canyon, and even the valley of Jackson Hole. The views were indescribable and filled us with a strong desire to go up into the mountains to explore.

After our boat ride, we spent several hours hiking the trails at the base of the Tetons. We climbed up in the rocks. It seemed that Nick (he was eleven at the time) was always in the lead, with Jordan (age five) following right behind. Those two had boundless energy, as did all the other cousins with us. We enjoyed a picnic in the Tetons and took in the gorgeous view of the lake and snowcapped peaks. When clouds moved across the sun, the light shifted, affording us an ever-changing view of the ageless mountains.

In Jackson Hole we decided to ride the alpine slide. Our family couldn't wait to enjoy sliding down a mountain again, and now those who had not been with us on previous trips could experience it for themselves. It's like sledding down a mountain but without the snow. You essentially race down 2,500 feet at speeds up to twenty-five miles per hour in the open air—no net. (Or maybe at three miles an hour if you're my mom!) It's exhilarating! Even my seventy-three-year-old dad and seventy-year-old mom joined us on the slides. Just like a kid, my dad excitedly yelled, "Yippee"—all the way down the slide.

WHITECAPS

While we were in the Jackson Hole area, we went whitewater rafting on Snake River. Seeing as our group had over twenty people, we were in multiple boats. My mom and dad were with our family. The rivers are rated based on level of difficulty using a scale of one to six, with six being the most difficult to navigate. Snake River was classified as a three, which is fairly dangerous, especially if you fall into the water. Even though my parents had never done anything like this before, my dad was just a big kid about it, raring to go; my mom, cautious as she was, said, "Tell that guide just to be careful."

The guide sat in the back while my parents, Marilyn, the kids, and I spread out evenly in the raft. The guide gave us a heads-up: "We're going to hit an area where it's pretty rough. Get ready." We got Jordan down in the middle of the boat and told him to hang on.

THE DISAPPEARING GUIDE

Sure enough, we came around a bend and hit the rapids between two big boulders. Boy, those waters were churning! We all started bouncing around the raft. We were in the thick of it when we hit a big rock. Our guide shot out of the boat like a rocket. He flew over our heads, splashing into the water about thirty yards ahead of us downstream! I was shocked and just tried to hang on like everybody else.

All of sudden, the guide was back in the boat. Surprised, I said, "How did you do that?" He explained that he'd grabbed the drag rope as it went by, yanked himself up, and popped back into the boat. It was unbelievable and a little scary, but he seemed fine. I was grateful for his experience, that he knew what he was doing, and that we'd put Jordan right in the middle to hold him down.

The kids jumped in the river a few times on the rafting trip, but in calmer waters. I can still see that guide flying up and over me. I'm sure glad he didn't miss that rope!

PRACTICING PATIENCE

After the grandeur of the Tetons and some time in Jackson Hole, we drove two hours to Yellowstone National Park to stay a few days. We knew it was big, but when we arrived and saw the vastness of the park, we were a bit overwhelmed. But we stuck to our plan to cover the major points of interest—all twenty-two of us!

My favorite moment was seeing Old Faithful again. It had been more than thirty years since I had been there as a child. As I watched our kids waiting for the geyser to explode, the forty-four minutes to an hour between eruptions didn't seem as long now. Yet, I had a pang of empathy for the kids. I remembered being young myself like that once—waiting, expectant, hopeful, and impatient! And then, POW! Old Faithful never disappoints!

Then we were off for the long drive around the park, stopping along the way to see Yellowstone Falls, Mammoth Hot Springs, Morning Glory Pool, and the wide, open fields teaming with buffalo, elk, and other wild animals. It was an experience like no other.

LOOK FOR THE ROPE

Have you ever been floating smoothly down life's river, feeling confident that you were following God's plan, only to be thrown out of the boat, trying to find the rope? I had been presented with an amazing career opportunity—one that would have been a big win financially. But there was one problem: I couldn't get a yes from God. Instead, He asked me: "What's your motivation?" I didn't want to answer because my motivation was money, prestige, and adventure. Then He asked me, "If I asked you to work at DaySpring for another year, ten years, or your entire lifetime, would you do it?" At this point, I felt like I had flown out of the boat—nothing under me, tumbling over the waves of my future. Reluctantly, I responded, "Yes,

LOOK AGAIN

God, if You want me to stay, I will." I turned the job down, grabbed the rope God offered me, and got back into the boat. Years later, God revealed the next assignment He had for me (leading DaySpring), which I would have missed had we moved for that "perfect" job. There's no doubt I'm exactly where He wants me, and there's nothing (not even all the money, prestige, and power in the world) better than that.

QUESTIONS TO PONDER

When you pray, do you try to convince God of your plans, or do you listen for His? How has God disrupted your plans for your life, and what did you learn from this? If He hadn't disrupted your plans, where would you be today?

CHAPTER 10

WHICH WAY?

MARK THE MOMENT

Back in those days, we didn't have cameras on our phones. We carried around cameras and cartridges of film—film that had to be dropped off for developing and picked up the next week. It was a whole process. I liked to mark the moment by taking pictures in front of every national or state park sign or any other point of interest. We had started this tradition during the very first trip we took. I'd stop and make everyone get out and smile—or at least try to. Then it was "Back in the car! Let's go!"

After surviving the whitewater rafting experience on Snake River, our next stop was Glacier National Park in Montana. This was one of those trips where nothing went quite as planned. We lost our keys (several times), we ended up staying at a "resort" (a.k.a. broken-down cabins with broken windows), and we were almost attacked by bears. It's true. I couldn't make this up! We thought we had made foolproof plans, but our plans don't always line up with God's, right?

The glacier-carved peaks and valleys, pristine lakes, and stunning vistas kept us uttering a constant stream of "Wow, wow, wow—take it all in!" Inspired by the views, we took some amazing hikes—we had over seven hundred miles of trails to choose from. We'd get curious and wander off the trails to walk down the glaciers with ten-to-twenty-foot drops in between, then we'd jump across them. Looking back, we might have taken some crazy risks since we were so emboldened by our many hikes and the stunning views.

SIR, DO YOU HAVE A PROBLEM?

After traveling up a treacherous road to Logan Pass (the highest elevation reachable by car in the park), we decided to take a hike and have a picnic. The views were breathtaking, especially in the cold, crisp air at an elevation of up to 6,680 feet. Since the hike was going to be somewhat strenuous, my brother-in-law, Jerry, and one of his sons decided to drive on to see other sights and then head to the motel.

As they were getting ready to leave, Jerry began to look for his keys and discovered they were locked in the car. You have to know this about my brother-in-law. He is a very organized, put-together, college professor guy. He likes everything in its place, and he likes things to go just right. We ended up calling for a park ranger to unlock the car. Luckily, this was not a new experience for the park ranger, and he had the special tool for the job. He unlocked their car, and they were off to their next destination.

Hours later we were at another lookout point and found Jerry there. He said he had locked his keys in his car again and was waiting for the park ranger. We all had a good laugh and headed to dinner in St. Mary, a small town on the outskirts of the park. After dinner, we were loading up the cars to head for the motel, and lo and behold, Jerry had locked his keys in the car a third time! Another call to the park ranger. Upon his arrival, the same park ranger said, "Sir, do you have a problem?" This was one of the most humorous things I had ever witnessed—not only because the keys had been locked in the car three times but also because it was *Jerry* who did it! I thought nothing could be funnier than that ... until we arrived at our lodging for the night.

OUR "RESORT" STAY

Looking at the guidebook, my brothers-in-law picked a lake resort. We'd planned to take the seven-mile hike up to Salamander Glacier the following day, and this looked like it was pretty close. It sounded perfect.

Since Jerry opted out of most hikes, he and his sons, Marcus and Anthony, decided to drive on ahead and get to the cabins early. He said the place was off the road on the right after the main highway. So, since we were coming up later, I was following his directions, driving along in the middle of nowhere, keeping my eyes open for a resort with the other cars following me. When we drove past a few tired, old buildings, I thought, *That can't be it, can it? Nah.* But there was nothing else for several miles, so I circled back.

Sure enough, that was it.

The name, it turned out, was overly generous. The "lake" was a pond so shallow and small you could jump across it. The "resort" was just a few rundown cabins—the worst I'd ever seen. There were windows, but some didn't even have glass panes. "Don't they know there are bears out here?" someone asked.

Unbelievably, after experiencing all that natural beauty,

here we were with very crude accommodations. At first, I felt angry. I thought, *This isn't a resort, it's a dump!* We'd been hiking all day, though, so it was too late, and we were too tired to look for someplace better. We just decided to make do. My crew went from cabin to cabin to find the best of the lot, and we finally settled on one. My sister Mary and her family took the one that had a door but had the window out, so we filled it with a piece of cardboard!

At least they have indoor plumbing, I thought. We had to take turns showering in a three-by-three-foot metal shower you could barely step into. Jerry lay down on the bed in one of the cabins, and it caved in. The worse and worse it got, the funnier and funnier it became. My anger slowly melted away, and pretty soon I was thinking, *Alright then, we'll make some memories here we'll never forget.* We ended up making a campfire that night and laughing until our sides ached. It's amazing what a change in perspective will do!

The next day, I woke up jazzed for our big hike up to Salamander Glacier—the whole reason we'd stayed in the dumpy cabins. Most everyone was so tired from the previous day of hiking that they elected to sleep in. Only two others actually got up and did that hike with me. Everybody else decided to stay behind and take it easy at the "resort."

FORK IN THE TRAIL

I'll never forget that seven-mile hike up to the glacier. The ascension is something like two thousand feet and fourteen miles round trip. To say the least, it was a difficult hike. Along the way, Amy, Randy, and I met up with a couple who were also determined to hike all seven miles. It's some dangerous terrain, but we wanted to see Salamander Glacier up close, which meant heading to the top.

Along the way, we came to a fork in the trail. Each branch went up another three miles before connecting again. This couple we'd met took the fork to the right, and we took the left. We wished them well, hoping we'd see them where the trail meets up three miles later.

Before leaving that morning, we had been warned to watch out for bears. We met up with a park ranger who advised, "As you walk, keep talking and making noise, and if you have a bell, ring it some." About two hours later, we arrived at the point where the trail joins up. We didn't see the other couple, but we didn't think much of it. After all, it was a very difficult hike, and many who tried it would turn back at some point. About an hour later, we heard the sound of a helicopter overhead. We wondered if someone had fallen or if they were looking for fires.

At the top, we took time to enjoy some lunch, take in the views, then we took pictures with the snow in the glacier that's in the shape of a salamander. After we went back down, we met up with some people who said, "Did you all see the helicopter? Some people on the mountain got attacked by a bear and had to be airlifted out." Chills ran up and down my spine. The couple we'd parted ways with had been attacked!

The next day, on the cover of *USA Today*, we read, "Couple attacked by bear in Glacier Park." So, it was true. We said a prayer for them, hoping they'd be okay. While I had wished for my entire family to make this hike with us, I realized what a tremendous danger they potentially avoided simply by electing to sleep in at the resort. It might not have been what I wanted at the time, but I was glad they hadn't come along. When we got back to the cabins, the place looked so different to me. The day before I'd seen it as a disappointment; now I saw it as a safe haven

> *The day before I'd seen it as a disappointment; now I saw it as*
>
> *for my family.*

for my family. It's all about perspective—always! I hugged

my family extra tight that day.

GOD HAS A PLAN,
AND IT'S NOT MINE

In 2017, I returned to that trail up to Salamander Point in Glacier Park. I hiked a few miles and met the ranger who'd been there twenty some years earlier during the bear attack. When I told him our "near miss story," he shared that he was the one who had to get those folks out of the park. It's incredible to me that on that particular day, we just happened to pick the trail to the left. I don't know why that couple was attacked and we weren't. This experience continued to cause a paradigm shift in my prayer life. Why wasn't it us? My only answer is God has a plan, and it's not mine. For example, I lost my best friend, David, at the young age of thirty-four. Even when I don't understand, I

LOOK AGAIN

have to trust that God is working His plan. He sees a bigger picture than we do. To this day, I wake up every morning and start the day with this simple prayer:

"God, You have a plan today, and it's not mine. I've got things planned today, but You can move anything on my calendar. Help me to be watching and listening, and then obey."

QUESTIONS TO PONDER

When your expectations don't quite match up with how things happen, how would choosing thankfulness or acceptance improve your perspective? How does knowing that "God has a plan, and it's not yours" help you view your circumstances differently and rest in the fact that He's all-knowing and you're not?

CHAPTER 11

JUXTAPOSITIONS: OREGON DOWN THE CALIFORNIA COAST

We only really grow through hard times. Now, I wish that wasn't true! I enjoy ease and comfort, but God uses hardship and struggle. He was growing me in major ways during this first trip without David, my best friend who lost a short battle with cancer the year before. And my mind was spinning with so many questions for God. *Why didn't You answer my prayers and heal David? Why did You take my friend away, God? Why did You take away Amy's husband?*

It had been a little more than a year since we had lost David. So, when we started planning the next year's trip, we thought about all the national parks in the Northwest. We decided to plan this trip primarily around Amy. We wanted to spend time with her and her family and try to plan some fun activities and sightseeing. It also gave us time to revisit some of the things we had done together up there—all just part of the healing process.

Like Marilyn, Amy had come to college at John Brown University in Arkansas. Marilyn had come from Wyoming and Amy from Oregon. David fell in love with Amy, I fell in love with Marilyn, and the four of us became best friends. We had so many adventures together over the next twelve years.

On this trip, Amy took us exploring around Oregon, and we reminisced. During this time, we had hard questions for God. We didn't abandon our questions, and we didn't pretend they weren't there.

However, I remember a conversation we had one evening after dinner where the Lord helped us gain some perspective. We talked about a statement that one of our other best friends, Dean Kerns, had made when he lost his wife Ruth to cancer a few months before David died. He said, "I am not going to let the things I don't understand about God determine what I do know about God." We

> *I am not going to let the things I don't understand about God determine what I do know about God.*

slowly decided we would not give up on God; instead, we would rejoice and celebrate the eleven and a half wonderful years David and Amy were married and the wonderful times we had enjoyed during those years. To this day, the joy Amy exhibits is an amazing testimony, even though it's something we will not fully understand until eternity.

On many more occasions throughout this trip, I found myself asking *Why?* over and over. The answer I always got was "It's not for you to know." The more I thought about it, though, the more I realized that maybe I was asking the wrong question.

I was on a faith journey, one where God was pointing out all the places in my heart that weren't surrendered to Him. And truthfully, the question *Why?* was all about me. *Why did You take my friend away? Why did You do this to me?* As we learned in the last chapter, it's not about me—it's about *His* plan. So, I shifted my question and started asking *What? What are You doing, God? What is the bigger picture, and can I see it?* Asking *Why?* was getting me nowhere, but when I started asking *What?* God started revealing His plans to heal our hearts through one amazing trip, starting with devastation and ending with a castle.

TURNING POINTS

The most memorable stop we made was at the very massive and active stratovolcano Mount Saint Helens, where the deadliest and most destructive eruption in American history happened nearly a decade before. Even after all that time, the devastation was incredible. The eruption sent ash into the sky some fifteen miles high, killing fifty-seven people. The forests were flattened for more than one hundred square miles around. We even experienced the effects of the eruption over two thousand miles away in Arkansas—ash in the skies over our heads. As we neared the area, we became reverently quiet. The sounds of nature were eerily still. It was a humbling experience. We were all somber. I looked around thinking of how this single event caused so much distress and sadness. I thought of how so much can turn on a dime: the phone call with unwanted medical test results, the receipt of a pink slip, an eviction, the loss of a pregnancy, the death of a relationship. In every case, someone was whispering, "I'll never be the same." It was a lot to process, especially in light of David's recent passing.

Even so, I realized that this devastated landscape would

eventually heal. That's God's design. He redeems all things. As the Word promises, "For I am about to do something new. I have already begun! Do you not see it? I will make a pathway through the wilderness. I will create rivers in the dry wasteland" (Isaiah 43:19 NLT).

If I truly believed that God would eventually heal this land, this wreckage, then I had to also believe that He would heal my wounds, my wreckage. God is in the business of restoration—it took me seeing the destruction left behind by a stratovolcano to recognize that there's always more "wow" with God. This land would eventually be filled with greenery and flourishing with wildlife again—I could just picture it! And I would eventually be filled with peace and deep-seated joy at the mention of David's name.

DEEP WATERS AND RUGGED BEACHES

The energy level cranked up when my sister and her family joined us to start another adventure. We headed south along the Oregon coast, stopping along the way from Cannon Beach to Bandon Beach before making our way to Crater Lake National Park, which is actually a lake in a sleeping volcano. This thing is over two thousand feet deep—the deepest lake in America. We hiked up the volcano and stood looking over the rim. It was amazing!

We traveled down the famed Highway 101 along the Oregon coast, then darted to Highway 1 and continued down the California coast. While it's a coastal drive, it's rugged, not beachy. We drove along looking out over splendid cliffs. It's a bit like driving on a bridge with the water constantly in sight. As a child, I'd seen these same views from the rear window of our old Buick. Now here I was, living out my childhood dream of being in the driver's seat while my own family took it all in. I admit it felt like a lot more responsibility than I'd anticipated. One wrong move could have been devastating. With some effort, I relaxed and enjoyed the beautiful drive.

Northern California has gorgeous vistas and forests of oaks, sycamore, walnut, pine, and laurel, among others. The variety of trees truly astounded me and reminded me of how creative God is.

After many hours in the car, we arrived at the tranquil Redwood National Park, home to the world's tallest trees. These redwoods have very long lives; some are estimated to be over two thousand years old! The tallest redwood, at

379.7 feet, rises higher than the Statue of Liberty. We took lots of pictures to show how tiny we are by comparison. It was like being in a grand cathedral where everything about it pointed your attention up, up, up, and into the heavens to the Maker of all things.

BAYSIDE

We'd spent a lot of time in rural areas during this trip, exploring the great outdoors. Soon we began moving into the more cosmopolitan part of the trip. When we got close to San Francisco, we were all excited. That said, we were still on a budget, so we rented motel rooms outside the city to save money.

It had been many years since I had been to San Francisco. Like my father before me, I wanted to take my family to that magnificent feat of engineering—the Golden Gate Bridge. We made our way downtown to see the sights and explore the massive city. The Victorian row houses and steep hills gave the city a quirky flavor. We got a glimpse of Candlestick Park, the stadium where the 49ers and Giants played.

CASTLE ON THE HILL

We then proceeded south along the coast, stopping at Carmel-by-the-Sea to take in magnificent views of Big Sur. A few hours later, we ended up at Hearst Castle, a fortress formerly owned by media mogul William Randolph Hearst and now in the care of the state of California. The property is on a quarter of a million acres, high on a hill. It took nearly all the next day for us to tour this place, which makes sense considering it took upwards of thirty years to build it. There are lots of outbuildings, but the "big house" has over thirty-eight bedrooms, all decked out in the finest of finishes and furnishings. It's an American castle, to be sure.

This amazing place wasn't just a house—it was practically a city! It had more resources than a small country. The best part for me was the most enormous, grand swimming pool I've ever seen—and there's one inside and one outside! I thought of how thrilled we'd been when Dad booked us that motel room with the six-foot-deep pool when we were kids. We'd had the best time in that thing, and you could have fit fifty of them in this one pool! What would young James have thought of this beautiful monstrosity? And what would Hearst have thought of the motel pool?

WHY, GOD? WHAT, GOD?
ASKING THE RIGHT QUESTION

This trip taught me about the magnificence of God. Overlooking the death and devastation that had taken over the Mount Saint Helens landscape was a somber experience. Then we traveled down the coast where we witnessed so much life in the gorgeous vistas, the redwood trees, and the coastline. It was a journey from devastation to life; it was as if God was using this time to show us that we would live again and He would restore our hearts. Seeing God's grandeur in the beach was soothing, calming, and reassuring, and it drew us back into our faith.

In life, we'll all face rough seasons. And trust me, the struggles don't go away with age—they just keep coming. Along the journey, I discovered

LOOK AGAIN

that changing my question from *Why?* to *What?* altered my perspective. Asking *What?* instead of *Why?* changes my focus from looking at my current circumstances to looking up at what God is doing through my circumstances. It shifts my focus from my plan to God's plan. We all have problems, but God is more than enough to help us through them when we place our eyes and attention on Him.

QUESTIONS TO PONDER

How does it make you feel knowing that God redeems and restores all things? What place of destruction can you release to God, and in so doing, open yourself up to the new thing He wants to do in you? How would asking God *What?* instead of *Why?* help you find more peace and clarity?

CHAPTER 12

ONE HISTORIC TRIP

Like my dad, I have a healthy respect for our country, and I wanted to share that conviction with my kids. Taking them to visit our nation's capital was a priority for me. Since I traveled a lot for my job, it allowed me to accrue hotel points and airline miles. So, for two or three years, I saved up enough points to take our family on what I like to call *One Historic Trip*.

Visiting the historic sites like Arlington Cemetery gave me and my family a deeper and more profound respect for our soldiers and country, but it also gave us a different perspective on life. There's more to this life than what we can see. With my eyes, I saw hundreds of white crosses signifying the losses we endured as a country. But as a Christ follower, I was also keenly aware that this world isn't the end. God had a plan for each one of those lives just as He has a plan for yours and mine.

THE CAPITAL

When summer vacation arrived, we flew to Washington, D.C. Our first stop was George Washington's historic home, Mount Vernon, on the banks of the Potomac River. Being there and taking the tour gave us a sense of what the home life would have been like for the general who became our nation's first president. His father died when he was eleven, so he helped his mom manage the farm; it was here that he learned the importance of hard work. He never attended college or received any formal education, yet God used him in such a big way. God does that! He takes ordinary people like George Washington, like Uncle Ervie, like you and me, and He works through them to do unimaginable things—things like starting a new country, pouring joy and generosity into your family, or becoming a leader of a company. At one point, all these things

> *When God is involved, nothing is impossible.*

didn't seem possible to the people who attempted them, but—I hope you hear me on this—when God is involved, nothing is impossible (Matthew 19:26).

After visiting Washington's home, we headed to view

the sights in Washington, D.C., most of which I'd visited as a teenager. My kids were close to the age I had been when I first visited our nation's capital. This time I experienced the same sense of awe I'd felt on that first visit as I viewed the impressive skyline with the enormous Washington Monument and surrounding iconic landmarks.

I knew from experience how much it helped to have an inside look at our government, so I'd contacted our senators and our house representatives to get tours and tickets for everything. I wanted to really unpack the structure of our government and how it has withstood so many challenges over the last two hundred years.

Walking into the capital and the two chambers and taking in the weightiness of it all left us with a reverent feeling of awe and gratitude. There's no other country like ours! We're a self-governing republic that voluntarily gives power to our elected representatives. And these representatives are just normal people like you and me. While I had learned this as a teenager on my group trip to Washington, DC, I wanted my kids to understand it as well. I wanted them to see the inner workings of our government up close and to take it in. It's one thing to learn about it in history class; it's a whole other thing to be sitting in the actual space where our country operates. I was overjoyed to see my kids fully amazed by our nation's systems and the people who run them.

GRAVITAS

Then we made a visit to the Lincoln Memorial, that imposing sculpture depicting a stoic Lincoln. Most of us have seen the statue in films, but when you're there, it's impossible not to feel the gravity he must have felt. A humble man, Lincoln governed during one of our nation's darkest and most divisive periods. Being there and letting that sink in affected us all deeply.

Next, we went to Arlington Cemetery, 639 acres of land where those who have served our nation with dignity and honor are buried. Seeing over 400,000 white crosses filled my heart with gratitude and reverence. We visited the Tomb of the Unknown Soldier there at Arlington and observed the changing of the guard ceremony, which occurs every thirty minutes. The monument honors the unidentified dead from past and present wars. It was an impressive and somber ceremony, and we experienced this moment with total strangers who were from all different backgrounds, affiliations, ages, and races—and yet, it's as if we all had the same heart. No one moved or spoke, but as a united group, we all felt the weight of honoring these soldiers who lost their lives for our country.

We drove from there to Gettysburg, Pennsylvania, where the defining battle of the Civil War was fought. I always like to explore significant historical sites whenever I travel. This was a special visit because we paid tribute to the more than 58,000 men who died in the battle that took place over three horrible days; it was a sobering visit. Looking out over that field, I couldn't help but think about all the soldiers, their families, the lives that were impacted by their service.

WILLY WONKA

As we drove toward Philadelphia, we decided to take a break from visiting historical sites with a visit to Hershey, Pennsylvania. This place is a kid's dream come true—chocolate fountains, a full amusement park with fun rides, and every type of chocolate under the sun. And boy, were we ready for a lighthearted moment! The chocolate factory gave us a space to drop our shoulders, laugh, and have a little fun. So, we took this Willy Wonka moment and ate it all up! And you know what, I'm pretty sure God was smiling as we rode every ride at Hersheypark with our hands high in the air.

HISTORY IN THE MAKING

Now, I hadn't picked the cities we were visiting out of thin air. I was intentional about wanting to see the three original seats of our nation's government: New York City, Philadelphia, and Washington, D.C. New York City was the first capital of the United States. Philadelphia is home to our nation's first and second Continental Congress, and in the postrevolutionary period it was the temporary capital of the United States. Then the Residence Act in 1790 put the capital in current-day Washington, D.C.

We toured Independence Hall, where our founders met in the 1770s and 1780s. That's where we saw the famous Liberty Bell with its signature crack. They used to ring it to call lawmakers to meetings. It's inscribed with a verse I know well: "Proclaim liberty throughout all the land unto all the inhabitants thereof" (Leviticus 25:10 KJV).

TEMPORAL VS. ETERNAL PERSPECTIVE

As I reflect on the history of our country, I'm sobered by both the *greatness* and the *sadness*: the greatness of the many challenges this country has overcome, and the sadness of all those people (soldiers) who were lost and never recognized. The gravity of visiting their graves really made me think about my impact on the world and how temporary my life is. We really don't have much time here, friend. God has placed each of us here at this time and place for a specific assignment. He's given us each specific gifts and abilities to fulfill our role in His amazing plan. Even on the days when we wake up and think, *Not again,* we keep going because we have work to do. In fact, we *get* to do work! We have the opportunity to get in on

LOOK AGAIN

what He is doing. Doesn't that just blow you away? The Creator of the universe doesn't *need* to involve us, but He chooses to! He wants a real and personal relationship with us, and He allows us to participate in His plans. It's our choice whether to join Him on this great adventure.

QUESTIONS TO PONDER

What would change in your life if you lived each day as if it were your last? How would shifting your focus from the temporary to the eternal change your goals regarding your relationships, health, or future plans? How is God asking you to use your gifts and talents to expand His kingdom?

CHAPTER 13

SURPRISE!

MANHATTAN

God loves to surprise and delight us. I'm absolutely convinced of it (Psalm 37:4)! Why else would He have made the sun, the stars, the mountains and oceans, the sunrises and sunsets? He is an amazing Creator! And that's the tip of the iceberg—just think what He has for us in heaven! Know what else I'm convinced of? Because I'm made in His image, surprising and delighting others is built into my DNA and is one of my favorite things to do.

From Philly, we took a train into New York City. This was the first time the kids had ever been on a real passenger train, so they were really excited, but I was even more thrilled. Why? Because I knew what was next. I didn't tell them the train was going to drop us off in Grand Central Station

> *God loves to surprise and delight us.*

in the heart of New York City.

When they stepped off the train, their jaws dropped. They weren't quite sure where they were, but as we started our way up the stairs and into the main part of Grand Central Station, they were awestruck—it was written all over their faces. Actually, so was I. The beauty of the building and its sheer size are overwhelming, and it's mesmerizing to see the thousands of people that come and go through the station. The intricate design, artwork, windows, and flooring are an amazing work of art and architectural wonder. But the best thing my eyes drank in was watching my kids' faces light up in wonder.

After twenty to thirty minutes, we made our way out and caught a taxi to the hotel—another surprise. I had used points again and reserved a room at the Marriott Marquis on Broadway and West 46th Street. I had requested a room overlooking Times Square, and I was fortunate to get one on the thirty-ninth floor. It was stunning to look out and see all the lights and excitement of the bustling city.

Taking in New York City for the first time with our kids was a thrill. We walked the streets, took subway rides, did the Circle Line tour, and rode a ferry out to the Statue of Liberty on Ellis Island. Upon returning from Ellis Island, we went to tour the World Trade Center. We went by Wall Street, viewed the Brooklyn Bridge, and then stopped at the Empire State Building for a ride to the top; the panoramic view of Manhattan was spectacular. We topped off the day with dinner at Tavern on the Green in Central Park.

With the trip wrapping up (or so everyone thought), I had one more big surprise while we were in New York. Many years ago, on my very first business trip to New York City, I had a small booth at a trade show. I had two spinners to show off all of our finest DaySpring products, and I stayed in the cheapest motel I could find. One night, I was taking a stroll around the city and walked down to Rockefeller Center. I discovered one of the most unique and coolest stores I had ever been in—Teuscher Chocolatier. It is a small, fancy chocolate shop. All the confections are made in Switzerland and flown to New York each week!

Intrigued, I went in and looked at all the beautiful chocolates. Then I peppered the clerk with questions: Which ones are the best? Which is the most famous? How much are they? She graciously answered each question and highly recommended the champagne truffles. I tried one, and it was exceptional! But they were four dollars apiece. *Whew! That's a lot for two bites of a truffle!* But I bought a dozen and took them home to my wife and daughter (my boys like them too!) I was a hero. It was the best fifty dollars I ever spent. They were so good—melt-in-your-mouth good. From then on, whenever I'd visit New York City on business trips, I'd bring home champagne truffles. On this day, we walked into the shop as a family, and they could finally see and experience where I had been getting these delicious treats. Even better, they could order whatever they wanted. What a delight for me to watch as they enjoyed the chocolates right there in Rockefeller Center!

PINK SANDS

Like my dad before me, I had one more trick up my sleeve before our trip was over. I surprised the kids with a flight from New York to Bermuda. I went all out on this one. You should have seen their faces when they found out! They were just a little more than excited, and Marilyn and I were pretty excited too! And I've got to tell you, my heart soared—things like this give me great joy! In fact, giving brings way more pleasure than receiving. And of course, Bermuda didn't disappoint. It's an amazing place!

The water was crystal clear, and the sand was

remarkably pink due to tiny bits of coral and crushed shell mixing with it. We were able to use my Marriott points to book rooms in a hotel right on the ocean; it was an exceptional experience. Our kids made friends on the beach, and we lived it up for a week. Riding mopeds around the island was a ball. We enjoyed dinners out at nice restaurants. I even got to play a couple of famous golf courses there. Our kids were growing up and were starting to appreciate more. This was unlike our usual budget (pop-up camper) trips, thanks to our accrued points. Instead, this trip was a shock to our senses, just as I had planned it to be. I kept all the surprises in my back pocket and pulled them out one at a time, and I was thrilled because they were thrilled. Like I said, enthusiasm is contagious. And I like to surprise and delight.

SURPRISE AND DELIGHT

I'm a hopeless romantic. I've gone to great lengths to bring joy to those around me, especially my wife. Reenacting our first date at Pizza Hut or our backyard proposal brings back special memories. I love to surprise and delight her and others. Sometimes it's a big trip, but usually it's small and simple like a $4 champagne truffle; both work and delight those around me. Plus, I've found it really hard to get down in the dumps when I'm focused on surprising and delighting other people. It takes energy to love and surprise others, so I work at finding ways to fill my own tank. I have some wonderful friends and mentors and they help me find the right perspective. Not to sound too cliché, but I also work at delighting myself

LOOK AGAIN

in the Lord (Psalm 37:4) by spending time with Him. It sounds easy, but it still takes work, focus, time, and discipline. It's a muscle you have to develop and practice daily. I've discovered that truly delighting in the Lord happens when I sit and clear my mind with my Bible, a journal, and a pen. And when I've finished, I'm better prepared to go about my day with the right perspective.

QUESTIONS TO PONDER

What are some ways you can surprise and delight those around you today? How would surprising someone you care about help to improve your own mood and attitude? In what ways has God surprised and delighted you lately? How do you fill up on God's love so you have enough to pour out to others?

CHAPTER 14

MULES IN THE CANYON

'm not very good at sitting still. I think most people would say that I have quite a bit of energy. And the truth is, sometimes I go full speed at something without putting a lot of thought into it. Oftentimes, I'll go into projects feeling confident and courageous, but when I don't think them through enough, I end up feeling frustrated. Every time I hit an unforeseen obstacle or realize that I should have planned better, I'm hit with a good dose of humility. This trip was filled with obstacles and doses of humility, and what I found is that it's better to admit defeat and walk away rather than try to keep pressing on no matter what the outcome.

> *It's better to admit defeat and walk away rather than try to keep pressing on no matter what the outcome.*

RACE TO THE RIVER

When my dad took our family to the Grand Canyon all those years ago, I'd been awed by the sheer size of it. The Grand Canyon itself fills the horizon for as far as the eye can see. At over 270 miles long and eighteen miles wide, it's the size of a small state. It's also a mile deep. Back then, we ran around a bit and explored, but Dad called us back far too soon. I was determined that my family and I would really take it in this time.

When we went to Grand Canyon National Park, we'd already talked about how we wanted to hike all the way down. The Colorado River called to us with something like a siren call. And now that we were in the heat—it was nearly one-hundred degrees—the roaring waters below held endless appeal.

We watched as a tour guide led a group on mules onto the trail; they seemed to amble along as slowly as a pack of sloths. I said, "What do you think, guys? Should we ride the mule or go on foot?" We'd taken a lot of mountain hikes by then, and we decided we could make better and faster time on foot. "Alright then," I said, never wanting to waste a minute. "Let's go!"

The AAA guidebook promised a 5,000-foot descent to the very bottom. First you hike down 3,800 feet to an overlook; then the last 1,200 feet are like a switchback to the Colorado River. That's not even a mile-deep descent, but it's a six-mile hike each way. We were fairly confident we could do that.

As we took off, we were all laughing, each of us excited for the adventure. We had a total of eleven people with us on this trip, including Amy and our friend Janie, and we were certain we'd made the right choice. We were hot, but we were dressed for summer, wore comfortable shoes, and had sunscreen on. (The three girls—Marilyn, Amy, and Janie—were the exception. They had decided to wear these matching overall jean shorts and lime green shirts; they looked cute, but as it turned out, their matching outfits were not good for the hike back up the canyon. But that's another story!) We had individual water bottles to keep hydrated, and we planned to be back before dark. All would be well.

Abbey and Marilyn took their time walking along with their friends, just chatting and having a good time, while my sons and I hit the trail hard. Always looking for the thrill, Jordan began running down the hill with Nick in pursuit, like always.

The boys and I kept up a good pace while keeping a keen eye out for mule droppings. We passed those folks on mules going down. I thought, "We're doing great! If we'd ridden those mules, we'd never make it to the river." The trail was dry, rocky, and uneven, but it was well-worn. The switchbacks along the cliffs were steep, but it would be fine. We just needed to take our time.

OVERLOOK COMPROMISE

At about 3,500 feet down, there's a place where you can refill your water bottle and rest. And it's a good thing, too, because my bottle shrank in size on the trip down. It seemed huge up on the ridge, but I'd finished that little thing off in the first half hour. It was so hot! It had taken us two and a half hours to get to that point. Another hour down meant we'd be making the entire trek in seven or eight hours.

I had to admit that we might have bitten off more than we could chew. Admitting that I may not have thought this through hit me hard. I didn't like the idea of not finishing the entire hike to the bottom, but our later start limited our choices. Sadly, I had to let the group know that we probably needed to head back if we wanted to get back before dark.

The adventurer in me wanted to go for it! But it was best to call it and start heading back.

My group agreed. They were even thrilled with the idea. It wasn't what we'd planned, but it was good enough. We hung out at the edge of the cliff for a while so we could see the river below; we took some pictures and congratulated ourselves on what we'd achieved. Truth be told, we were really having a ball. It was a pretty incredible experience.

GOING UP

As we headed back up, Nick and Jordan took off again. They were all energy, just like their dad.

Marilyn, Abbey, and our friends had stayed together and also started their journey back up to the top. I felt torn. I wasn't in any hurry, but I didn't like the idea of the boys up there alone in the wild. It was Nick's job to stay with Jordan, and usually that was a good fit, even though it was a lot of responsibility. I didn't like them being out of my sight, so I started to coax the girls, "Come on, we can do this!" But they were getting tired and were in no hurry. They said, "Will you leave us alone? We're focusing on walking and just trying to breathe!" Truthfully, we were all breathing heavier, and we were all tired—everyone except the boys, that is. We'd drunk most of our water, so we were thirsty too. And the heat wasn't letting up one bit.

We quit talking.

The terrain that had seemed merely interesting going down seemed especially rough going back up. I thought, "This is more dangerous than I'd anticipated. I hope the boys are okay." Right about then, I heard the sound of hooves behind us. The folks on mules passed us on the way up! I realized then how much more slowly we were going on the way up. I picked up my pace and left the others behind so I could catch up to the boys.

The hike back to the top had taken me four hours. I was exhausted but exhilarated. Nick and Jordan had been waiting for over an hour. Nick said it had taken them two and a half hours from the overlook. They'd started to worry that we were lost. I laughed and assured them the others would be up soon.

Twenty minutes passed. Half an hour. An hour. I was really starting to get worried about the girls. As the minutes ticked by, I watched the trail opening with something akin to dread. I tried not to worry, but it was getting late. It was twilight.

After five hours and fifteen minutes, the women emerged from the trail. One after another—fifty feet apart—not even together. They were sore, tired, and unhappy. It was the most they could do to focus on breathing, putting one foot in front of the other, and not falling on the rocky trail. They spotted us, gave us a chilling glare, and walked silently to the SUV. I was thrilled to see them, but when I started to say so, it was clear none of them were ready to hear that yet.

I drove us the two hours back to where we were staying. The conversation in the Suburban was very limited, and at times it was completely quiet. The hard feelings were still too fresh, and our attention was on our tired, aching muscles. We arrived close to midnight and immediately took turns soaking our sore bodies in the hot tub. All you could hear was the weary silence and maybe a sigh of relief.

We continued on our journey and had more wonderful adventures, but weeks passed before we could talk and really laugh about the Grand Canyon hike.

====== LOOK AGAIN ======

SILENCE IS
SOMETIMES THE BEST CHOICE

It's pretty humbling when mules pass you by. You've been there, right? You've made a decision, you're feeling confident about it, you start going down that path with bravado, and then you start to look around and realize maybe it wasn't the best idea. At this point, you can do one of two things: you can either keep pushing on, knowing that it's not right, or you can swallow your pride and turn around. It's hard to admit when it's time to throw in the towel, and it's hard to face people (especially naysayers) when what you had so passionately planned didn't work out. However, I've learned more from the humble moments in life than from my successes. These

LOOK AGAIN

moments of humility require dependence on God, and this is where confidence begins. It's what I call the "principle of the opposite." Need courage? That comes during moments of fear. Need patience? That comes during moments of trial. Need confidence? That comes during moments of humility. Don't get down when life teaches you some tough lessons. Some of the hardest things we go through are God's best gifts. So don't dread or fear the hard things—just do your best to be prepared for them.

QUESTIONS TO PONDER

How do moments of humility force you to depend on God? How can you embrace humility as a teacher instead of letting shame set in? In what ways have difficult experiences actually been gifts from God to help you learn important lessons?

CHAPTER 15

NAVIGATING THE RISKS

Life is a participation sport; it's not suitable for spectators. We navigate the risks, we push through the obstacles, and we might even be surprised by a few storms along the way. But does that mean we let fear take the reins while we hide from the unknown? Absolutely not. We seize the day, we prepare the best we can for the bumps, we take risks, and we persevere.

We've all been at a crossroads before—we feel compelled to move forward, but fear surfaces and persuades us to stay put. It presents the same old argument—it's not safe. As if that weren't enough, fear convinces us it wouldn't make a difference anyway. But that couldn't be further from the truth. In fact, I've found that taking the right risks has helped me and my family grow in courage and confidence. Not to mention, it helped us place our trust in the One who is ultimately in control, and it gave us a front-row seat to the most beautiful views in the world. This trip was full of scary, sometimes downright dangerous experiences, but it was also full of mind-blowing moments of God's beauty—beauty we would have missed if we hadn't taken the risks. And I don't want to miss it! I don't want my wife and kids to miss it! I want to take it all in, mark the moment, and live it out!

I drove a Chevy Suburban that summer with a pop-up camper in tow like the old days. It had an air conditioner and was bigger than my dad's, but it was still nothing fancy. I spent the whole time on this trip reminding my kids, "This is what I did when I was eleven. This pop-up is nice, though, isn't it?" There were too many of us to all sleep in the camper, so we planned to put up a tent too. We also slept underneath the camper overhangs in our sleeping bags in the open air on the bare ground.

BOYS IN THE LEAD

We'd learned about a rock formation called Angels Landing at Zion National Park that promised an incredible hike with a huge payoff at the top, along with bragging rights for having made such a dangerous climb. It's an exposed hike up an enormous rock 1,500 feet above the canyon floor. In many places, the only thing between climbers and a deadly fall is a chain rail bolted into the rock. If you're afraid of heights, this isn't for you.

Our drive to the trail was full of expectation and pent-up energy. When we finally arrived at 9:00 a.m., Jordan and Nick jumped out of the Suburban and took off up the mountain path—they were gone. Marilyn looked over at me and said, "James, you've gotta keep up with these kids. This is too dangerous for me to watch!" I had barely put my keys in my pocket, and already they were out of view. I had to get going!

I took off after the boys with the rest of our group coming behind at a slower pace. I was going fast, trying to catch up, but the views slowed me down. I had to take it in! The beauty of the sunshine filtering through the moving clouds gave the mountain range a constantly changing color palette of pinks, peaches, oranges, and yellows. Patches of green trees and canyon grasses spilled out of crevices, defying the rocky terrain. I hadn't yet caught sight of Nick and Jordan even though I was moving quickly, nearly running. I couldn't see the others behind me either.

The path zigzagged and continued to narrow. The rocky cliffside hemmed me in. The drop off the steep narrow spine tested my fortitude. I thought, "This is scary dangerous." I began to worry. What if the boys fell? What if I fell? What if one of the girls fell? My anxious thoughts weren't helping. "Lord, protect us," I prayed. "And deliver us safely back to each other." I focused on my breath and making each step firm and strong. My heart rate stayed high, and my muscles burned, yet I no longer felt any anxiety. I felt peace and awe.

It takes most folks about two and a half hours to reach the top. I had made it to the top in about an hour and a half, so I was winded. When I arrived, both boys were there, taking in the views, smiling like the cat who ate the canary. "How come it took you so long?" they asked. Nick stated that he didn't catch Jordan until he got to the top. They were so impressed with what they'd achieved and how they'd beat everyone to the top. We high-fived and gazed at the amazing views in all directions—rock formations in incredible hues, rocky mountains and boulders as far as the eye could see.

About forty-five minutes later, the others joined us. I had brought some extra water and snacks in my backpack, so we shared a little lunch up there together, snapping photos and saying, "Wow, just take it in." Marilyn was especially glad to see that everyone had made it safely to the top. She was glad I went on ahead so she didn't have to watch the boys speeding up the rocks. It stressed her out. She asked Jordan if he'd been scared. He said, "No way! Scared of what? It was awesome!" He was just fine.

We were learning that with each trip, our kids' courage grew. I think our threshold for risk was also raised. Staying engaged in the adventure made us feel so alive. In fact, we discovered that one courageous act led to another courageous act, and we were growing in confidence too. Courage begets courage. I could see it in my family. Life is full of adventure, and we were experiencing it firsthand. And while that included taking some risks, our eyes were open to God's majesty through the beauty of His creation. We were growing and *truly living.*

THE NARROWS

Another challenging hike we made in Zion National Park was in the Narrows. The mouth of the Narrows is pretty wide—a quarter mile across or so. The first mile is fairly easy. Then it narrows to maybe fifty to one hundred feet as you go farther into the canyon. Then it narrows down to fifteen or twenty feet in some areas. The Virgin River flows through the canyon, and hikers must wade back and forth across the river multiple times on the journey. It gets two or three feet deep, even waist-high in some places, but on this day, it wasn't moving too fast. I'm tall, so I hung on to our kids to help them safely across. After that first crossing, we hiked on dry land farther into the canyon, then had to cross back over again. While it was probably one hundred degrees elsewhere, in the canyon it was at least forty degrees cooler.

It was a sunny day, so rising river water hadn't concerned me, but park rangers warned us about flash floods. Desert soil can't absorb water quickly, so when it rains upstream, even one hundred miles away, runoff drains into the valley. It can multiply ten times the volume of the water coming through the canyon! Walls of water can rush through the canyon, getting as high as fifty feet, engulfing everything. Park rangers informed us that hikers had been swept away over the years.

This wasn't a theme park; it was raw, powerful nature. We had to be cautious. Skies may be clear for thirty miles, yet a rainstorm elsewhere had the potential to wipe us all out. I felt like I was on high alert.

Halfway into the hike, we heard it might be raining upstream. I felt a little nervous about this news, but after we spoke to a ranger in the area, he assured us that everything would be just fine. They were monitoring the situation so we didn't have to. We continued for a few more miles before deciding to turn around and head back. Of course, we made it out fine or I wouldn't be here to tell the tale. But that threat of rain in another county kept me on my toes, braced for danger. It was a thrilling and beautiful hike, but it was nerve-racking—even more so than hiking up Angels Landing. Not being able to see ahead and what might be happening upstream made me a little uneasy.

Water can be full of surprises. Rock, on the other hand, is predictable, unchanging … or so it would seem.

SOLID AS A ROCK

Bryce Canyon National Park is home to some incredible rock formations. Much like the Badlands, it's an intimidating landscape, with an other-worldly feel. Except for the reassuring scent of blue spruce and Douglas fir, it's like landing on a different planet where you're not sure you'll be welcomed!

We spent about four to five hours at Bryce. I'd never seen anything like the hoodoos there, which are tall spires of rock that are like naturally formed chimneys. We could even see what looked like the edge of the Grand Canyon from some of the high lookouts. Our favorite part was exploring the "natural bridges," which are arches formed by millions of years of water, wind, and frost erosion. Can you imagine the power it takes to erode solid and seemingly impenetrable rock?

Emboldened by our adventures at Angels Landing and the Narrows, we set out on an eight-mile hike. The difference here was instead of climbing up, we descended into a rock metropolis of hoodoos and spires surrounded by sweeping sandstone walls. Because of the loose, sandy soil, we really had to watch our footing. On our way out, we walked along an astonishing vista and had an unbelievable view of Thor's Hammer, an imposing and isolated hoodoo. We continued to journey along these enormous rock formations and took some fantastic pictures. What an experience!

Let's pause for a moment and talk about the risks we've taken so far on this trip:

- We went on an exposed hike up an enormous rock.
- We hiked through a narrow canyon that could fill up with Virgin River water on short notice.

- We descended into a rock metropolis of hoodoos and spires.

Yes, we were taking risks, but nothing would prepare us for what came next. Sometimes you just can't avoid the danger.

DRIVING INTO A STORM

This was July, so it was hot, hot, hot and just as dry as could be. One day we were driving across the desert when we saw a rainstorm coming. I said, "Oh, good! We'll get a break from this dry heat!" We could see those clouds contrasting with the bright sunlight from what seemed like a hundred miles away. As we drove toward it at a bit of an angle, the clouds were gathering and growing in intensity. The sky was filled with unbelievably beautiful colors. The clouds and colors continued to grow in size, and just when I thought it couldn't get any more gorgeous, lightning began to strike in the clouds. The display of power nearly took my breath away.

At some point I realized, "Wow, this thing is getting a little close." I'd never experienced anything like this and wasn't sure what to do. The highway went on for miles and miles with no shelter; there was only desert on either side of the road. We got to a certain point and realized we were going to run straight into the storm. The rain bounced off the pavement ahead of us. The sky was changing, getting darker and darker. And then it happened: we drove into the storm. The winds blew so hard I had to grip the steering wheel hard. We were pulling that pop-up camper behind us; it was lurching back and forth causing the Suburban to rock side to side.

Excitement and awe turned to anxiousness. Yet, after a few minutes, we safely drove out of the storm. What a relief! I released my death grip on the steering wheel and began to relax a bit. Then I looked to the left and saw a wall of water moving toward the road ahead of us. It had rained uphill a few miles or so away, and all the water couldn't be absorbed by the ground. This wall of water, which was at least ten or fifteen feet high, was rushing down into the valley, and we were heading right toward it. It was coming toward the highway fast, so I decided to speed up. I was in a race to beat this thing before it crossed the small valley ahead. Thankfully, we beat it, but barely! Once we got up on the hill, we turned back to see that wall of gushing water go right across the road where we had just been.

Our kids talk about that experience to this day. The truth is, sometimes you see the storm coming, and sometimes

> Sometimes you see the storm coming, and sometimes you don't.

you don't—some risks are just unavoidable. When the storms of life come, we have a choice: we can either stick it out or we can fall to the pressure. Building courage is so important because it helps us persevere during the tough times. Life is full of moments that aren't fantastic, but we can't quit—we have to keep going. We must look forward and ask, "What will God be up to next?"

COURAGE BEGETS COURAGE

Life is full of adventure, and we should fully live it. Be willing to put yourself out there and try a few new things. Test it out, learn from it, and grow in confidence. And if you fail, grow in humility. Either way, you grow, you learn, you *live*. You can prepare for life, but part of the preparation is understanding that there are unknowns in your future. That doesn't mean you sit on the sidelines—get out there and play the game! So many people give up or settle, but God calls us to be strong and courageous (Joshua 1:9). Whether we take calculated risks or not, storms will come our way, and we'll have to make decisions. Will we go backward, stay put, or move forward? When we're facing uncertainty (let's face it—we're *always* facing uncertainty), we can be afraid of what's ahead or excited about it. When we fully embrace the concept that God is in control and He has our best interests at heart, then we can release all our doubts, concerns, and worries about the future and spend our time wondering what awesome opportunities He will reveal next.

QUESTIONS TO PONDER

What kinds of storms has God helped you walk through? What lessons did you learn about God and yourself after the storm passed? Are you naturally courageous or timid? How would taking more risks help you act more courageously? In which areas of your life do you need to walk in more courage?

CHAPTER 16

FIRSTS: LAKE POWELL AND THE RAINBOW BRIDGE

We've slept in all kinds of places during our years of travel—roadside motels, with and without pools; tiny, rundown log cabins with no windows; lakeside retreats; even elegant hotel suites.

We slept in sleeping bags outside or in the pop-up camper after following those mules up the trail in the Grand Canyon. Now we drove northeast from Flagstaff for a new adventure on Lake Powell, a reservoir on the Colorado River. There we would travel nearly two hundred miles by boat. And not just any boat—a sixty-five-foot houseboat.

There were eleven of us on this particular trip—my family, Amy, our friend Janie and her sister and family—all on this big boat. For a full week, there was nothing but us, rock, water, and a few straggling bushes for miles and miles. I mean, we were in the middle of nowhere, and we were limited on things we could do. We didn't have cell phones, restaurants, or even grocery stores. And at first, it was a strange feeling to be surrounded on all sides by barren, rocky cliffs. But after the "strange" subsided, I found the undistracted time with family to be very fulfilling. Because our entertainment options were limited, we were forced to concentrate on our relationships and surroundings. We became closer as a family and friend group, and we had plenty of time to marvel at God's amazing creation. I will always remember the night sky—it was unbelievable! The millions and millions of stars that lit up the darkness left me in complete awe of God and His magnificence, and I had time to sit in that feeling because there was nothing else to do.

> *The millions and millions of stars that lit up the darkness left me in complete awe of God and His magnificence.*

COMMIT

We planned to travel the length of the lake, as much as two hundred miles, to see the sights. That's quite a commitment!

We'd have to bring everything we needed for the journey, as there were no stops along the route. There were only two marinas at that time about fifty miles apart, so we had to plan wisely in case we needed supplies or fuel. And it was crazy hot! Daytime temperatures hovered around one hundred degrees, but at night temperatures dropped to a pleasant sixty or seventy degrees.

At one point, we happened to see another boat anchored close to the cliffside. We watched as these folks scaled the cliffs, then jumped into the water from what looked like fifty to one hundred feet in the air. We cheered and clapped. The kids blurted, "We want to jump off those cliffs too!" I said, "Let's join in!"

Well, that was easier said than done. First you have to jump out of the boat because you can't get too close to the cliffs. Then you have to swim one hundred feet to the cliff and find a place to safely climb up. Scaling those cliffs was tough. You'd be wet from the swim, and the cliffs were slick. Water shoes helped. As you moved up, the cliffs were dryer, but this was free-climbing—there were no steps or anything to stop your fall. Finding the right foothold in the rock outcroppings was crucial. Then a strategic jumping-off point was critical to avoid hitting the rocky ledges on the descent. When I got to the top of that first cliff, I looked down and had no way of knowing how high it was. Three, maybe four stories high? There was only one way down: run and jump!

I jumped.

Whoa! What a rush! I stayed below treading water and offering encouragement and direction while the others climbed and jumped. It was insane, but once we'd jumped, each of us was hooked. We loved it!

We jumped and dove for hours.

The next day we did it again. We cliff-jumped from dozens of locations, dozens of times. Each time the risk seemed less scary. Simple run and jumps. And the boys even started doing some flips. We'd hold hands and jump together. We would all dive off at the same time. What would have seemed crazy just days before became normal.

THE BENEFIT OF LIMITATIONS

We were stuck in those sandstone canyons together for seven days. The only way out was to traverse on and around the entire two-hundred-plus miles of water. We dove, we swam, we jumped off cliffs, we water skied (thanks to a ski boat that Janie's brother-in-law brought). In fact, Lake Powell is where Abbey and Jordan learned to ski. When we found a little spot of shoreline, we'd anchor and go onshore to explore. Some evenings we would build a campfire. We prepared and ate all our meals together, and we relished every bite. And while I'm normally always on the go, wanting to see the next thing, I found that the change in pace was enjoyable. The limitations forced us to slow down, refresh, renew, and just be—and that was something we weren't used to.

Finally, we came to Rainbow Bridge, the largest natural bridge in the world. It's an inspiring natural stone arch that rises almost three hundred feet into the air. It's as long as it is high. It's beyond amazing! You can take your boat up close, but then you have to walk the last half mile because the water is so shallow. So, we made the trek on foot to get an up-close view.

REMEMBER HOW BIG GOD IS, HOW SMALL YOU ARE

My kids would tell you this was one of their best family vacations ever. It's a memory we will never forget and always cherish. I think it was so memorable because of their age and because we were together with nothing to do but enjoy God's creation. There is something special when you are out away from everything and experiencing something for the first time. "Firsts" are the best! When you gaze up at the stars, you are reminded that He spoke everything into existence, and placed us on a tiny planet called Earth. It gives us perspective and reminds us how big God is, and how small we are; yet, how amazing is it that He—the Creator of the universe; the One who made

=========== LOOK AGAIN ===========

every star, every rock, every blade of grass—wants a

real and personal relationship with me and you. Now

that is a big idea, and it's true!

QUESTIONS TO PONDER

When is the last time you stood in awe of God's

creation? Or had a new experience? Or opened a

window and felt refreshed by the sun? Are you

allowing yourself time to slow down and take it in?

Are you giving yourself opportunities to enjoy the

vastness and beauty of God's creation?

CHAPTER 17

LAKE SUPERIOR? COUNT ME IN!

I love taking a team across the finish line. The truth is I want to take as many people as I can with me on every journey I take. To say I'm a "people person" is putting it lightly. Helping others see what they can't see in themselves is one of my greatest joys in life. It gives me energy. When I see a person, I see their potential, I want them to succeed, and I want to be a part of their journey. I want them to experience God's *wow moments*.

> *Helping others see what they can't see in themselves is one of my greatest joys in life.*

By the time we were planning our next trip, word had really gotten out. And before we knew it, over twenty people had signed on for the adventure.

Needless to say, I was thrilled. We had activities planned every day—hiking, biking, canoeing, boating, golfing, fishing—anything a family of adventurers would ever want or need. The best part? Some friends of ours in Minneapolis offered us their cabin a few hours north of Duluth, which was close to not one but *two* national parks! We jumped at the chance.

LOCATION, LOCATION, LOCATION

Their "cabin" turned out to be so much more than I could have imagined. It was over six thousand square feet and had three levels of luxury. When we arrived, we were all blown away. The cabin's back door was about fifty feet from Lake Superior. To this day, it's still one of the most beautiful settings I've ever experienced in my life. The coastline is ruggedly beautiful. We loved sitting outside on the deck, especially at sunrise and sunset. We used the cabin as our home base from which to venture out to Isle Royale National Park in the northern part of Lake Superior and Voyageurs National Park located outside International Falls, Minnesota.

EXPLORING

We were just three miles from a little ski community called Lutsen. Only about two hundred people live there year-round, but it swells in the winter when skiers arrive. It's situated at the base of a two-thousand-foot mountain that looks out toward Lake Superior. We discovered an alpine slide in Lutsen for us to all go sliding. Dad and Mom joined us again. Dad was eighty years old, and Mom was seventy-seven, but they were still game to ride the slide. We drove four-wheelers and paddled in canoes on Lake Superior, where the average depth is 535 feet.

We went up and toured the Grand Marais and Grand Portage area and took a boat from there out to Isle Royale National Park. It's a three-hour ferry ride to the island, which is approximately forty-five miles long and eight miles wide. There are four lighthouses on the many shallow, rocky reefs that line the shores.

We went on big hikes to various waterfall areas. We went on a guided trout fishing trip, catching a few ten-to fifteen-pound lake trout. We went into the nearby towns and did tourist things like shopping. We played golf. We swam. We did it all.

HOME BASE

While this was certainly an activity-driven trip, we made sure to slow down every morning and evening as we prepared and enjoyed breakfast and dinner together. We called the cabin on the lake our "home base." While I loved all the action, I have to say that "home base" was such a blessing. It's where I got to connect with people, celebrate the day's activities, hear how everyone's day went, and encourage them to go even farther the next day.

JUMPING IN

One day as we were hiking at one of the state parks about twenty miles away, we saw a little bridge in the distance. It crossed over one of the rushing streams coming down from the mountainside. We looked down about thirty feet to the rushing water and spotted two young guys (maybe twenty years old) standing on the ledge of the bridge. They were taking turns jumping into a little narrow crevice into a pocket of deep river water. This crevice was approximately twelve feet wide. One would jump in, then disappear for a minute. I'd hold my breath, straining my eyes to catch sight of him again, and then there he'd be, climbing back up. Then the other guy would take a turn.

Next thing I knew, Nick and Jordan had joined them. I shouldn't have been surprised. We'd done some cliff jumping before in Lake Powell, so in their minds, this wasn't much different. I started yelling, "Guys, I don't think that's a good idea!" but they couldn't hear me over the rushing water. Moments later I saw them flying down into the cold water. They loved it! They climbed back up and did it again. They must have jumped in half a dozen times. Getting out was a bit difficult because they had to get out on the precipice and hang on to a protruding rock or something. The two guys had shown them it could be done, and that settled it—nothing could stop them.

Had they not had the experience at Lake Powell where they became comfortable jumping off cliffs, they probably would never have had the courage to jump into this river. Because it was so narrow, they needed the prior experience to ensure that they jumped from the right spot.

This is even more proof that courage begets courage. My boys never would have had this adventure if they had not already experienced jumping before. And witnessing the other guys' courage increased their own.

WHAT JOY LOOKS LIKE

This trip was different. The thing I liked best about it was how our evenings were so restful. Fixing meals and eating together at the cabin soothed our souls. After going at full throttle all day and then having a nice meal, I'd go out and rest right at the water's edge, even dozing at times out on the smooth rocks. This wasn't just a vacation; it was an experience of deep, lasting joy I could draw on for days and years to come.

WE ALL SEE THINGS DIFFERENTLY— AND THAT'S A GOOD THING

My joy was multiplied by taking others along on this adventure. This time we each traveled at our own pace and did only the activities we wanted to do. It was all about welcoming folks to experience adventures while also having open hands and allowing them the opportunity to sit this or that one out. Some ride the brakes a little harder than others, and that's okay. Not everybody is going to have the same level of courage or risk. They're each on their own journey.

I try to connect with people where they are— total strangers, family members, friends, coworkers, servers at restaurants. I desperately want them to know that God created them not only for this time and place but also with unique abilities and experiences

LOOK AGAIN

on purpose so they can do the amazing things He's called them to do. What's the best way to get this across to them? By loving them well. The key to creating real impact in the lives of those around you is by letting them know through your words and actions that you genuinely love and care for their well-being. Once they know that, you can share anything with them. The door's wide open.

QUESTIONS TO PONDER

What was your last courageous act? How have you become more courageous over time? Which specific actions have led to the growth of your courage and confidence? How can you help someone in your life see a bigger version of themselves—a more courageous version?

CHAPTER 18

RETHINKING WHAT'S POSSIBLE IN HAWAII

D ream big" is a popular phrase that seems to be popping up everywhere these days. Similarly, there's "Reach for the stars," "Make it happen," and "Believe in yourself." There's nothing wrong with these phrases; in fact, I've probably used them a time or two myself. The danger in these phrases, though, is that they put the emphasis on what *you* can achieve but neglect to mention that God can take you so much further than anything you could accomplish on your own. With Him, *all* things are possible.

> God can take you
> *so much further*
> *than anything you*
> *could accomplish*
> *on your own.*

In Matthew 19:26 it says, "Jesus looked at them intently and said, 'Humanly speaking, it is impossible. But with God everything is possible'" (NLT). Let me repeat that—*everything is possible.* There's nothing He can't do.

Think about that—there's not one thing off the table when it comes to God. He can make anything possible— know it, trust it, and believe it with all your heart. You can "dream big" all you want, but you can do the impossible when you're aligned with the Creator of the universe. This next trip opened my eyes to God's vastness, gave me insights into what He is capable of, and grew a heart of gratitude in me.

DREAMING BIGGER

Since my big wake-up call earlier in life when I decided to live as if I were called and not driven, my family and I had logged thousands of miles and seen more national and state parks than I could have ever imagined. It had been ten years since we launched into this adventure. The kids had grown up, and we were nearing a new season in our family.

We were on the cusp of a new adventure. Nick was all set to graduate from high school, and Abbey would follow close behind. I felt it was time to dream even bigger, so we saved up and splurged on flights to a destination that would have seemed crazy to consider just a decade before: Hawaii.

As on so many of our previous trips, we invited friends and family to come along. My brother Jonathan, his wife, Christi, and their three kids came too, along with a couple of Abbey's and Nick's friends—extended family members, as we called them. Like I always say, "More folks, more fun!"

NOTHING IS IMPOSSIBLE WITH GOD

Flying over the Pacific Ocean at 38,000 feet, I thanked God for the gift of allowing me to take my family on a trip of a lifetime. The flight from Los Angeles to Honolulu would be over five hours on a nonstop flight. Incredibly, it had taken my dad two weeks on a boat to get from Honolulu to San Francisco when he came home from World War II. Our five-hour flight seemed like nothing compared to that. I had big plans over a two-week period to visit three islands: Oahu, Maui, and the Big Island. We had worked out our lodging for approximately four days on each island.

As we stepped off the plane, greeters met us in Honolulu with smiles and traditional Hawaiian leis, garlands of local flowers. I could hardly wait for more "firsts" for all the kids and their friends. We were all ready to experience everything the islands had to offer. But I could never have been prepared for what was ahead. God really blew me away this time.

IN MEMORIAM

Our first stop was Pearl Harbor, the site of that infamous surprise military strike by the Imperial Japanese Navy that killed 2,403 Americans on December 7, 1941. We took a short boat ride to see the site of the sunken ship, USS *Arizona*. The memorial sits on top of the sunken ship. It's really quite somber and peaceful there. Nothing could have prepared me for that moment, looking down into the depths of the sea, thinking of all those soldiers who died there. Our visit to the Pearl Harbor Memorial reminded me of the precious gift of life. It helped that we had so many teenagers in our group—it was a sobering, hands-on lesson about the costs and impact of war.

GLORIOUS SIGHTS

We drove next to the North Shore where big thirty-foot waves were the norm. We watched the surfers in amazement. We enjoyed a traditional Hawaiian luau, celebrating with music, good food, dancing, and lots of laughter.

At Diamond Head State Monument, we hiked the slopes of the fantastic volcanic crater. At the summit, you can see for miles and miles. On Maui, we went out on a whale-watching expedition, which was unbelievably beautiful. It's quite a thrill when these huge, glorious creatures burst out of the ocean, flipping their tails as if they were greeting us. Our boat got right up close to them. It seems odd that such large creatures could live so close to land, and in fact, they rarely come close to the continent of North America. But in Hawaii, you're basically in the middle of the Pacific where the water is so blue and the waves are intense.

We splurged on a helicopter ride, too, which afforded us incredible views of the islands. Our guide recounted for us the wonderful origins of these islands—how they'd been formed over centuries by the eruptions of volcanoes. They rise over 33,500 feet from the floor of the Pacific Ocean, with some of the islands 10,000 feet above sea level. Again, it occurred to me that nothing is impossible for God!

Creation didn't just happen. When you take in these views and learn about how the islands came to be, you can't help but see God, because there's just no way this beauty happened by itself.

REWINDING FOR A REPLAY

Again, I relished our evening meals best of all. Gathered around the table, spent and hungry, we shared our different experiences of the island. The mix of adults and kids made for spirited conversations about their various observations of the day. It was almost like we got to experience the day's events all over again, seeing them from each other's viewpoints. We had great debates, too, because we were all so energized and in such a happy atmosphere. It's hard not to have a good time when you're in Hawaii!

One of my other favorite meals while on Maui was at the outdoor restaurant at the hotel. It was facing west, so as we ate and talked, we were able to watch the sun drop into the evening ocean. That night the kids wanted to try some more new things. I ordered five different appetizers, including some sushi and very rare ahi tuna along with wasabi paste. Watching their reactions was priceless. Jordan really liked the ahi tuna. I ended up requesting three more orders because we all liked it so much. We had octopus, too, which felt rubbery to me, but it was just fun to try something new. The fourteen of us around this big table had a great time.

During this trip, God reminded me that He's made

us all different from each other. He gave us different life experiences, different likes and dislikes, and different ways of thinking. And you know what? He did it on purpose. Think about that for a second. He created every person, every personality, every mind, every soul—and He loves them all. To me, a bologna sandwich on a mountainside is as good as a five-star meal when you're enjoying it with the right people at the right time. Of course, we won't always see eye to eye on everything. But sharing life, sharing beauty, and sharing experiences with others brings a richness that's not possible alone. God made us different on purpose, but He also made us for community.

ULTIMATE SUNRISE

I'm a big believer in rising early and watching sunrises, so I cajoled my group into making a predawn trek up to Haleakalā National Park. We had to wake up at two in the morning for the two-and-a-half-hour drive up. This is not an easy drive—it's a rugged volcanic mountain, dense with vegetation and palm trees in some places and rocky and barren in others.

At the top of that 10,000-foot mountain, we had a

360-degree view. In most places, even in the countryside, you can only see a little bit of the sky. Up on that mountaintop, as we looked around, it was almost dizzying. With no lights and no moon, it was very dark, and the sky was clear of any clouds. The panorama of stars was unbelievably intense. It felt like we could reach out and touch them.

Soon it was sunrise. It was sublime. I watch that same sunrise from my deck in Arkansas every morning, but this was "over the top." In my travels, I've seen the sun rise over the Atlantic and Pacific oceans, Lake Superior, Lake Powell, and so many other places. But at 10,000 feet, with nothing at all inhibiting the view, it is truly remarkable and impossibly beautiful. Clearly, God was showing off, maybe just for us.

That sunrise put it all in perspective.

Again, I was reminded of how small I am and how big God is. The same God who put the sun in the sky wants a personal relationship with *me*! He makes all things possible—and He doesn't really need me. He can do it all by Himself, yet He wants to be in my life. He wants me to share all my thoughts, worries, and concerns with Him. And He wants to fill me with all the joy, hope, strength, and wisdom that I need to get through this life. And He wants to do the same for you. How amazing is that?

LIFE FROM LAVA

Next, we flew to the island of Hawaii for our final Hawaiian adventure. It's called the Big Island because it's twice as big as all the surrounding islands put together.

We spent our days exploring the entire island. The terrain varies radically depending on the region. Kona is terrific for coffee growing with its rich, volcanic soil. In some places the beaches have black sand due to the volcanic material. While Kona actually means "dry," the other side of the island is wetter with glorious waterfalls and lush vegetation. We visited Pu'uhonua o Hōnaunau, another national park, which is plush with white sand beaches and coconut palm trees. It was absolutely gorgeous. We walked along rocky beaches where the huge ocean waves crashed heavily into the rock crevices.

At Mauna Loa—in Hawaii Volcanoes National Park— we experienced the largest active volcano on earth. We walked the surrounding trails and got to see molten lava flow out of the ground. We could walk right beside it! It was a gift to see the volcanoes at work, serving God's creative purposes. The island itself was being created before our very eyes as the lava spread out across the land, over the cliff, and into the ocean. So amazing! Approximately 2,500 miles from the nearest landmass anywhere, this volcano continued to create land on which flora, fauna, and people thrived. Steam rose as the lava hit the water and formed new land.

IT'S ALL ABOUT PEOPLE, NOT JUST THE EXPERIENCE

As I watched land forming before my very eyes, I couldn't help but think, *What more proof did we need that with God, all things are possible?* He set it all in motion. The rising sun and the emerging moon are perfect examples of how God takes care of us. How could it "just happen" that our bodies need rest for at least eight hours a day, and it "just happens" that our earth goes dark for about eight hours at night? None of this "just happened." God planned it, and He continues to plan things for us. All things are possible! Nothing's off limits! I often think of my first trip as a four-year-old boy, lying in the back window of that Buick. God (through my dad) encouraged my passion for adventure. That four-year-old boy never would have dreamed that a trip to Hawaii was in his future. The entire time I was in Hawaii, it felt too good to be true. It was like God put everything amazing in one place—the ocean, mountains, volcanoes, sunsets, sunrises, rock formations, coral, and colors. But without the people, the colors wouldn't have been as vibrant and the adventure wouldn't have been as meaningful.

QUESTIONS TO PONDER

What will you remember most about life—the adventures or the people? What would it look like to accept and celebrate others' differences? When you think about nothing being impossible for God, what impossible situation comes to mind, and how can you release it to God?

CHAPTER 19

FISHING IN ALASKA

I like my own ideas—until I hear a better idea. Learning to stay flexible and openhanded with my plans and ideas has helped me remain open to what God has in mind. I believe Corrie ten Boom said it best when she stated, "I have learned to hold all things loosely, so God will not have to pry them out of my hands." It's so easy to get caught up in *your* idea that you forget to listen for the *best* idea. And the best idea may not be yours! Personally, I've found that when I see God showing up in another person, or a different group, it's best if I just get out of the way and let it happen. And even if I didn't get to cross the finish line with them, I'm thrilled because I got to see God at work. Jealousy has no place in God's work. He is

> *Learning to stay flexible and openhanded with my plans and ideas has helped me remain open to what God has in mind.*

working in each and every one of us, we are all on a different path, and we should celebrate when we see God working through someone else.

Staying flexible and working together was instrumental during our trip to Alaska.

FISHERS OF MEN

When I was growing up in the church, I learned early on that Jesus hung around with lots of fishermen. That has stuck with me because I have always loved to fish.

My son Nick is the best fisherman in the family. I believe he'd be happy just to live in a tent and fish for the rest of his life. When Nick was ten, he came along with me on a two-day fishing trip on the White River in Arkansas. It was a balmy day in March; it was about sixty-five degrees, and we were out fishing. On the second day, we were eight miles upstream from camp when some clouds blew in. Then within a few hours, temperatures dropped about thirty degrees. It started to rain, and soon the rain became pellets of ice and snow. But the fish were still biting! The guide asked if we wanted to head back. Ten-year-old Nick said, "No, way! We're catching fish!" So, we laughed and stayed out for another three hours. We caught another thirty fish that afternoon! He was determined, even then. And he's a fisherman to this day. Now he loves to take his own twin boys fishing.

We'd been fishing a lot of places, but Alaska was always the dream. I'd done some research and decided to combine fishing with visiting some additional national parks, including Denali and Kenai Fjords. When I told Nick and Jordan the plan, they were pumped. I invited some others to come along but didn't have any takers. Even Marilyn and Abbey took a pass because they didn't have a lot of interest in fishing; besides, they wanted me to have some wonderful new experiences with my sons.

For this great adventure, it would be the three of us. Just three fishermen.

Outside Anchorage, Alaska, is the great Kenai River. It's possible to catch different types of fish depending on the time of year. We chose to go in July because we wanted to try king salmon fishing; these are big 40-to-70-pounders. But first, we wanted to fish the upper Kenai, the best place to fish for trophy rainbow trout. There were just four of us—Jordan, Nick, me, and a guide—in a big drift boat. The guide paddled while we cast for rainbow trout. The water of the Kenai is melted ice—glacier melt-off. It was so blue it was almost green.

The fishing was spectacular. At one point, a couple of huge moose waded across the river right in front of us. We were awestruck! These are huge, seven-to-eight-foot-tall animals. The guide quietly maneuvered our boat around them, and they acted like they didn't see us—moose are considerate that way. We caught some gorgeous rainbow trout in the upper Kenai. It was a serene, surreal, beautiful experience. The memory is etched in our minds. The experience was unforgettable, and up until that point, everything was going as planned.

FISHING IN A CROWD

After floating quietly along with our guide (and the moose) on the upper Kenai, I figured we'd be pretty much alone in the Alaskan wilderness, and we were. We saw only one other boat on that float trip. The next day was completely different. We got out on the lower Kenai where there were hundreds of boats anchored down, all angling for the big king salmon. This was competitive fishing! Our guide maneuvered our boat out into the fray, and we dropped our

199

lines into the water.

Then someone yelled, "Get out of the way!" And a boat barreled through the traffic on the water. You see, these salmon are huge—averaging fifty pounds and four feet long. They're so strong they literally pull the boat of whomever hooked them. A fisherman has to basically chase that salmon and wrestle it in or break the line. As a good sportsman, you don't tangle someone else's line. You have to pull up your line and get out of their way, and they'll do the same for you. So, while fishing might feel like a solo sport, you really have to be considerate of your fellow fisherman.

We figured out that if somebody on our boat hooked a fish, the rest of us had to quickly reel in our own line in case it was a big one. When they're big, sometimes you end up on a long boat ride chasing that one fish for up to an hour. The guide would yell, "Coming through! Make way!" This was happening with several other boats too. It was a free-for-all. If someone didn't get their line out of the water quick enough, the guide would slice the lines so they wouldn't get tangled. It was an unwritten rule, I guess, because all the guides had their knives out slicing lines while chasing the salmon.

So here we were, yelling at random fishermen as their

boats were being pulled through the water, dodging them left and right—not to mention if we weren't fast enough, our lines were sliced and we'd have to start over in a new spot. I had a decision to make: I could either get frustrated at the other fishermen for zooming by us and get angry at the guide for continuously slashing my fishing line, or I could see it differently. For the first time in my life, I started viewing fishing as a team sport. And it reminded me of my job. I know I shouldn't have been thinking about work while I was on vacation, but you can't help it sometimes, especially when you're so obviously on a team. If I was going to have a good time, I had to let go of my plans and my idea of a nice, peaceful fishing trip with my boys. I had to adapt, so I did. Those hard-won catches were really sweet.

I wasn't always so flexible, and it used to get me into a lot of trouble. I was sure my ways were the *very* best ways—*so sure* that when I was a young professional working for a start-up business and the founders called me into their office to tell me they'd sold the business, I was ticked. *How could they do this without telling me?* I thought. I actually looked them in the eyes and asked them why they didn't sell the company to me (even though I didn't have any money to buy it). And I remember the calm smiles on the faces of Dean Kerns and Don Leetch when Don looked at me and said, "We never really owned the business; it was God's business, and we feel God will do so much more if we open our hands and let it go." I didn't understand it at the time, but now I do. Thirty-five years later, DaySpring is still going. God had a plan.

SEASICK

After two days, we all caught 45-to-50-pound king salmon. It was a huge adrenaline rush for each of us! But we weren't done fishing yet. We wanted to fish for halibut, so we asked around and found a guide who knew where to take us. Little did we know it would be a two-and-a-half-hour boat ride to reach a drop off—a little cliff where the halibut liked to hang out. And we weren't fishing in a river now. This was the Gulf of Alaska (basically the Pacific Ocean). We'd taken motion sickness medicine when we went fishing that first day gliding down the Kenai, but after the smooth ride, we didn't think we'd need it anymore.

We had thought wrong.

The waves hitting our boat were enough to make me sick. We arrived at the guide's favorite spot, and I learned very quickly that halibut fishing is not a type of fishing you relish. It's something you endure.

Here's how it works: You cast a heavy line, almost like a rope, baited with a big piece of meat. You drop it about two hundred feet down to that cliff. Then you wait. And as you wait, the waves buffet your boat. When you get a bite, it's like a barn door is hooked on the end of that rope. You crank and crank until you can't crank anymore and then hand it off so someone else can take a turn. I'd hand it to Nick, and after he tired a bit he'd hand it to Jordan, and then he'd hand it back to me. I really loved the teamwork part of it. And as much as I wanted to brag about catching a halibut, the truth is, we all caught it. It was a team effort for sure.

The prize for all that wrestling is a huge but not very pretty fish. They're flat—gray on one side and black on the other. Even though they're ugly, they're one of the best fish in the world to eat. And at an average of one hundred pounds, one halibut is worth the effort because it goes a long way for a long time when you're feeding a family.

After three hours on the water, we'd each caught one. We were ready for the two-and-a-half-hour ride back to the dock. We were so happy to put our feet back on solid ground! We were also glad to have the experience behind us because compared to the actual event, talking about it later was way more fun.

ASKING FOR A FISH

I'm always trying to check off more national parks from our bucket list, so we put away the fishing gear and headed to Anchorage. From there it was a four-hour drive to Denali National Park, where we'd soon discover North America's tallest mountain peak, Denali, once known as Mount McKinley. At over twenty thousand feet above sea level, the mountain is sometimes visible from Anchorage, but not in its entirety. We wanted to see it all.

Denali National Park is huge—six million acres! We decided to take the sixty-mile bus ride into the park so we could take in the sights and maybe even see the big mountain up close. I have to admit, I was praying, "Lord, would You open it up so we can see these mountains?" Visibility was bad. It was raining. The guide told us there are really only about seven days a year when you can see Denali completely. I turned to Nick and Jordan and said, "Guys, let's ask God to open up the sky so we can see it."

I didn't like riding the bus along that bumpy stretch of

road. It was a slow go. I had no sense of how much time the journey would take. This time, I wasn't in the driver's seat, literally or figuratively. I did, however, have a window to look out, and that was interesting. I saw a gray wolf strolling along just looking at our moving bus, sizing up whether we were predator or prey. A moose ambled across the road causing the driver to stop while the great animal took his sweet time. Then a bear in the distance strolled across the tundra. We just watched in awe. After all, we were the guests here and not entirely welcome. Incredibly, some of the wild animals looked at us like we were there for their entertainment.

WONDER LAKE

Two hours into the ride, going twenty or thirty miles an hour, we came around a bend and arrived near Wonder Lake. I liked the sound of that, Wonder Lake. It spoke of possibilities. All of a sudden, the rain quit and the clouds opened up to big, blue skies. We could see the whole mountain with the beautiful lake in front. The guide who told us that it was only clear enough to view seven days a year was stunned. It was unbelievable. Snow covered the top half of the mountain as if it had been iced with sugar. Our mouths just dropped open. Everyone on the bus hopped off to take in the view. This massive mountain, reflecting in that crystal clear lake, was glorious. Camera shutters started clicking. My boys and I just stood there, and then I shouted, "Yippee, wow, God, You are amazing!" God had answered our prayer. We enjoyed that amazing view for about fifteen minutes. Those were precious minutes. Then the clouds rolled back in and visibility dropped, but we had seen it in its full glory! The rest of the drive we kept looking at each other and saying things like, "Can you believe we got to see that?" It felt as if that moment had been specially crafted just for us—like a gift.

ALL IN

We were absolutely lit up by that encounter. That night back at the hotel, I said, "You know, guys, I've read that you can actually take a small plane and fly over to Denali—fly all around it and even land at ten thousand feet. You can get out and look around. The trouble is, like today, we'll be at the whim of some tricky weather. Sometimes flights are canceled. Sometimes they take off, you get there, and the weather changes so you have to come back. What do you think? Should we give it a try? Take the risk?"

They looked at each other, then back at me. "Dad, we are *so* in! Can you make it happen?"

I got on the phone right away. I found a guide service that could fly us over to Denali and all around it. The next morning, we strapped in and prayed for clear, blue skies. The pilot cautioned us that bad weather can come in quickly. He had checked the weather reports just minutes before, but as we all knew, sometimes you see bad weather coming and sometimes you don't. After thirty minutes of flying, we were starting to get a close-up look of this icy mountain. We'd seen the whole stunning mountain from sea level, and now we were seeing it up close and personal from ten thousand feet in the air.

The exhilarating part of that trip was when the pilot was circling the mountain and began flying directly toward the side of the mountain. We could see those rugged cliffs coming at us fast! My heart began to race. The kids' eyes were like saucers. Then at the last minute, he backed away and continued around the mountain. Wow, what an experience!

OUR PERSPECTIVE IS LIMITED, BUT GOD'S IS NOT

Our perspective is limited. God usually only gives us our next steps, and we rarely get to see the whole mountain. We don't know exactly what lies ahead. But if we want to see more of what God has for us, we need to hold our plans loosely and not be afraid to take risks. Becoming too focused on our own plans can cause us to miss what God's up to.

Remember, your family, children, career, life, and day-to-day activities belong to God. Once you realize He's given you this time and place to make the greatest impact for His kingdom, it's easy to live open-handed without seeing the whole picture because we can trust that God sees it all and is working things

LOOK AGAIN

out for our good (Romans 8:28). Look again, friend.
Life is about trusting God, believing that He's for you,
letting Him guide you on this magnificent journey,
and bringing others along on the ride. A life full of
God adventures awaits.

QUESTIONS TO PONDER

What would it look like to let God be the driver or
pilot of your life? How can you actively trust God even
when you only see part of the big picture? How has
God cleared the clouds and opened up "blue skies" in
your life?

CHAPTER 20

SURPRISE AT YOSEMITE

t's important to make time for what really counts in life. In the past, I've let the wrong obligations and responsibilities consume my time. I allowed my busy schedule to get in the way of real-life moments such as family reunions and school activities. But through my trips over the years, if there's one thing I've learned, it's that I don't want to miss another opportunity to celebrate, encourage, and cheer on the people around me. It's not easy. Conflicts still happen, and I still miss out sometimes, but for the most part, I'm going to do everything I can to be there for the real-life moments.

THE SIXTIETH

It was my parents' sixtieth anniversary, and I wanted to do something really special for them. I had an idea: they had always dreamed of visiting Yosemite National Park, so I decided to make that dream a reality. My cousin Betty Jo lived in Sacramento and had been wanting us to come visit, so I worked with her and my siblings to put together a trip.

I asked Mom and Dad to come along; they were beyond delighted. My dad was immediately ready to go. Mom said, "Well, that sounds like fun." Once that was settled, my siblings and some cousins joined us to plan a surprise for Mom and Dad. We decided to make this a big family affair to celebrate this important milestone in their lives. Though they knew where we were headed, they were in for a surprise.

We flew in to the Sacramento airport, and after a few minutes there, I said, "Look, here comes Mary!" My parents lit up like candles. And then, "Oh, here comes Jonathan!" Then it was Robert, then David, and finally Jane! People kept showing up, and Mom and Dad were as surprised and excited as children at Christmas.

Now this is a real-life moment—one that I will never forget—and it was worth every single minute of planning and execution.

TAKE IT IN

Our first thrill at Yosemite was driving through Wawona

Tunnel. It's a hole cut through solid granite that's nearly a mile long. Being that deep inside the mountain is pretty amazing. Then at the mouth of the tunnel, there's a lookout spot with epic views—a breathtaking valley, enchanting waterfalls, and lots more. I used our walkie-talkies to remind the other van, "When you come through the tunnel, pay attention. We want to stop at that overlook. Otherwise, we'll have to go all the way down to the bottom of the mountain, turn around, and come four miles back up. Seeing it while going fifty miles an hour on the highway won't do. We have to stop and take it in!"

As we stopped at the overlook, most of us on that trip were seeing Yosemite for the first time. And you know I love being there for firsts! Watching the faces of people I care about come alive with wonder and delight is one of life's greatest pleasures. I looked around at the faces of these people I loved so dearly, considering how the daily choice my parents had made to stay faithful to each other and to God had led to this precious moment. It was a reflective and inspiring moment for me. *This is where I belong,* I thought, *surrounded by my loved ones overlooking God's beautiful creation and celebrating my parents.* I was beaming with gratitude. I could have stayed in that moment forever.

HEAVENLY CONFETTI

We drove to the Mariposa Grove, where there are over 500 giant sequoias, a few of them more than 3,000 years old and reaching heights of more than 200 feet tall. It was a crisp fall morning for exploring. After about thirty minutes of observing these mammoth trees, it started snowing. These were the biggest snowflakes I'd ever seen! Since there was no wind, they seemed to fall slowly and effortlessly to the ground below. What a nice surprise, as if heaven were celebrating with us! It was perfect timing. That light snow fell through the branches of these 200-foot trees, lightly blanketing the ground. We tried to catch snowflakes on our tongues like little children. It

> *What a nice surprise, as if heaven were celebrating with us!*

was beautiful. Though I'd planned the trip, I never could have dreamed of anything as beautiful as that. It made me smile and say, "God, You're amazing!" The snow melted a few hours later, as if it were a temporary party favor for our celebration.

In contrast to the gently falling snowflakes, the mighty rushing waters of Yosemite Falls came down in a deafening roar. All that water dropping over 2,400 feet inspired a sense of wonder and awe in each of us. My dad hollered, "Yippie!" That's what he did when he was excited. On this trip, he said it nonstop—"Yippie, yippee!" Here he was at eighty-one years old and my mom at seventy-eight, and they were still having the time of their lives. I was so happy that the people they loved were able to come along and celebrate this time together.

Out of all the trips, this one stands out because my brothers, sisters, nieces, nephews, and cousins made time to honor my parents. And while my parents have both passed, I can still hear my dad yelling "Yippie!" at the top of his lungs—I can hear it as if it were yesterday. Do you think I regret this trip for one moment? No way! There were so many reasons not to do it. We were busy, I had work, the kids were in school and involved in several extracurricular activities, and my wife was volunteering with countless civic and community organizations at the time. We certainly weren't sitting around waiting on something to do. But I wasn't about to let their sixtieth anniversary go by without a bang. It was important—more important than any deadline I had at work.

WHEN YOU GET THROUGH THE TUNNEL, PAY ATTENTION

I've driven hundreds of thousands of miles in my life, and when you're driving, you have to pay attention to the signs. If you don't, you'll miss your exit and end up at the wrong place. Life is the same way; you have to pay attention or you'll miss the wow moments of God. You have to pay attention, or you'll end up looking back on your life and wondering what you missed.

When I first started planning these trips, I had no idea how much I would get out of them. I was learning how to be *called* instead of *driven*, and I knew I needed to spend more time with my family. But once I hit the road, I discovered that I'd been missing so much. God showed me who He was through His creation, He

=========== LOOK AGAIN ===========

opened my eyes to the importance of making time for people, and I found myself astonished at His majesty. The more I saw, the more excited I became about what He had for me just around the corner.

Don't miss it, friend. Ask God to open your eyes, and then take it all in. Hold on to the beauty as long as you possibly can, and get ready to be amazed.

QUESTIONS TO PONDER

How can you be more intentional about stopping to enjoy the snowflakes? When was the last time you experienced a wow moment of God? How can you pay more attention to the people around you and help them experience wow moments of God?

PART FOUR

IF I ONLY KNEW THEN WHAT I KNOW NOW

CHAPTER 21

YOUR PERSPECTIVE MATTERS

Early in my career, I was working diligently to grow our greeting card business at DaySpring. I determined that we needed representation at the National Stationery Show in New York. I really wanted to take Marilyn, since she had never been to New York City. We needed someone to watch the kids, so I planned for us to drop off our kids at Marilyn's parents' house outside Cheyenne. Then I purchased airline tickets for us out of Denver. It all was working according to plan.

After the fourteen-hour trip to Wyoming, we got the kids settled. The next day, we drove three hours to Denver (on a seventy-degree late-May afternoon) so we could catch an early flight the next morning. We got to our hotel and settled in. I was so excited!

We got up the next morning and packed to go to the

airport, which was less than a mile away. I went to carry the bags to the car, and what a shocking surprise! It was snowing like crazy in late May! (We did not have mobile phones and weather apps back then!) It was snowing so hard that I could hardly see anything. There was already eight inches of snow, and it was still coming down. I was afraid I would miss this trip, so I scrambled to figure out a plan. After a few minutes, I noticed a person trying to dig his car out of the snow. When he finished, I asked if I could borrow his shovel. He obliged and I went to work digging out my own vehicle.

Four hours later, we finally arrived at the airport. (Remember, it was only one mile away.) I was a complete mess, frazzled and frustrated, almost ready to give up. It was still snowing, and no planes were leaving. We waited two more hours, and they finally called people to board the plane. An hour later, we were ready for takeoff! Finally, off we went, speeding blindly down the runway. We started climbing and climbing, and then, suddenly, we broke through the top of the clouds! There it was—all sunshine and big open blue skies! It was so exhilarating! After delays, struggle, frustration, waiting, and many unknowns, we made it! I remember saying, "Wow, God, You are amazing!"

For a while, I had lost perspective. Then God reminded me—there are always "blue skies," even when it's cloudy and you cannot see them. The truth is God is so big; He's over everything; He is always good and He is always there, just like the blue skies above the blizzard. All my strife and struggle to get on that plane, from digging the car out, to driving one mile in four hours, was all I could see in front of me. But when I rose above the clouds and saw the beautiful blue sky, my perspective changed.

> *There are always "blue skies," even when it's cloudy and you cannot see them.*

Keeping the right perspective can be difficult, especially if you are busy living life and running fast. And that's exactly what I was doing. I was one of those people (and when I'm not careful, I am still one of those people). Only when confronted with some hard realities and life-changing questions did I begin to "look again" and change my perspective, along with my actions.

If you are like me, much of life can feel pretty cloudy with "blue sky" moments few and far between. But if you change your perspective, or at least be willing to pause long enough in the midst of the blizzard to *look again*, I am certain you will find blue skies in God's master plan. And not only will your perspective change, but your life will change as a result.

God's plans are good. In fact, they are perfect. Scripture says He has a future full of hope for you. He loves you! You were created for a purpose. So, press in and press on! It's not easy, but it is good and worth the effort. I am cheering you on. God is cheering you on. He is ready to take you on an exciting adventure. Are you ready to go?

LOOK AGAIN

SEE WITH THE EYES OF YOUR HEART

My encouragement to you is to ask God to open your eyes and allow you to see the bigger picture. There is always more than meets the eye. Our circumstances cloud our way, but if we step back and ask God for His perspective, only then will we see with the eyes of our heart, and only then will we know what real hope is.

MY PRAYER FOR YOU

"I keep asking that the God of our Lord Jesus Christ, the glorious Father, may give you the Spirit of wisdom and revelation, so that you may know Him better. I pray that the eyes of your heart may be enlightened in order that you may know the hope to which He has called you, the riches of His glorious inheritance in His holy people, and His incomparably great power for us who believe" (Ephesians 1:17–19 NIV).

perspective

/pər'spektiv/

noun

1   a point of view.

2   a particular way of thinking about something,
     especially one that is influenced by your beliefs or
     experiences.

synonyms

outlook · view · viewpoint · standpoint · position · stand ·
stance · angle · slant · attitude · frame of mind · frame of
reference · approach · vantage point · interpretation

QUESTIONS AND REFLECTIONS FOR GOING DEEPER

CHAPTER 1

ORDINARY CAN BE EXTRAORDINARY

Exodus 4:10–12; John 10:27; I Corinthians 1:26–31

QUESTIONS

1. What are some benefits of coming from a humble background?

2. How often do you watch and listen for God's "wow moments"? What step can you take today to be more aware of what God is doing in and around you?

CHAPTER 2

ONCE YOU SEE GOD WORK, YOU NEVER UNSEE IT

Matthew 4:23; Philippians 1:6; John 5:17

QUESTIONS

1. Describe a fond memory from a past family trip. What made it so special?

2. Recall a time when God was working in your life but you didn't realize it until later. Describe what happened and how your eyes were opened to His work.

CHAPTER 3

IGNITE THE SPARK
THAT GOD HAS PLACED IN YOU

Romans 12:6–8; II Timothy 1:6–7; I Thessalonians 5:19

QUESTIONS

1. What sparks a fire in you? Leading others? Cooking a meal for someone? Building something?

2. How can you fan that spark into a flame and then a raging fire for God's glory?

CHAPTER 4

II Peter 1:3–11; II Chronicles 7:14; Romans 8:28–30

QUESTIONS

1. What's preventing you from letting go of your good and embracing God's best?

2. What is the difference between being driven and being called? And, what are the benefits and downsides? What things will indicate your call in Christ is sure?

CHAPTER 5

EXPECTATIONS VERSUS REALITY

Psalm 5:3; II Corinthians 5:17–20; Jeremiah 29:11

QUESTIONS

1. When was a time that your expectations collided with God's plan? How did you handle the disappointment, and what did you learn?

2. What does God's plan look like for our lives? What does transformation look like?

CHAPTER 6

LEARN TO LIVE "IN THE MEANTIME"

Colossians 1:9–12; John 15:1–5; II Peter 3:9

QUESTIONS

1. How would your life change if you processed the setbacks and slow-downs in life differently—embracing them instead of getting frustrated?

2. Are you usually ahead of God, behind God, or in step with Him? Explain. What are some practical things you can do to not miss out on God's plan and timing?

CHAPTER 7

SEIZE THE DAY!

I Corinthians 2:9; Ephesians 5:15–17; James 1:5

QUESTIONS

1. What are you doing today to make the most of the time God's given you?

2. How do you need to rethink your schedule or commitments so you can seize each moment—the quiet, uneventful ones; the exciting, big ones; and everything in between?

CHAPTER 8

THE FACADE OF CONTROL

Job 12:10; Isaiah 55:8–9; II Corinthians 12:9

QUESTIONS

1. What's the price you pay (physically, emotionally, relationally, or mentally) when you insist on maintaining control instead of releasing control to God?

2. How do you think your perspective of God would change if you released control to Him? How would your relationship with Him change?

CHAPTER 9

LOOK FOR THE ROPE

Joshua 2:1–21; Proverbs 16:3; John 6:35

QUESTIONS

1. What "ropes" has God offered to you, and did you grab hold of them? Why or why not? What was the outcome?

2. How can you remind yourself that the journey is more important than the destination? What's the most important lesson you've learned along the way?

CHAPTER 10

GOD HAS A PLAN, AND IT'S NOT MINE

Psalm 33:11; Psalm 40:5; Isaiah 55:10–11

QUESTIONS

1. How easy is it for you to surrender your calendar to the Lord to accomplish His plan? Explain.

2. Describe a time when you were disappointed about something only to come to appreciate it later. What caused the change?

CHAPTER 11

WHY, GOD? WHAT, GOD?
ASKING THE RIGHT QUESTION

Mark 8:34–38; Luke 1:26–38; John 9:1–7

QUESTIONS

1. How would understanding the magnificence of God more deeply strengthen your faith and focus on God?

2. How can we move the focus from "Why God?" to "What God?" What are the implications?

CHAPTER 12

... ETERNAL PERSPECTIVE

Ecclesiastes 3:11–22; Matthew 16:23; II Corinthians 4:16–18

QUESTIONS

1. How does it make you feel knowing that the Creator of the universe doesn't need to involve you in His work, but He does? How does this change your perspective and your purpose in life?

2. Which temporal things have been distracting you from living with an eternal perspective? How can you reverse this and focus more on eternal things?

CHAPTER 13

SURPRISE AND DELIGHT

Psalm 1:1–3; Psalm 37:4; Luke 10:25–42

QUESTIONS

1. Describe a time when it brought you more joy to give than to receive. How did you feel?

2. Why wasn't the Second Commandment first? What are the implications for us?

CHAPTER 14

SILENCE IS SOMETIMES THE BEST CHOICE

James 4:6–10; Isaiah 61:1–3; I Peter 5:6

QUESTIONS

1. What's a hard thing you went through that turned out to be one of God's best gifts? Explain.

2. Describe a time in your life when you were confident about your decision, but as time went on, you realized you'd made a big mistake. How did you respond—with humility or pride? What does humility cure?

CHAPTER 15

COURAGE BEGETS COURAGE

Joshua 1:5–18; II Chronicles 32:7–8; I Corinthians 16:13

QUESTIONS

1. When you're facing uncertainty, how do you usually respond—with courage and excitement or fear and anxiety? Explain.

2. What does being strong and courageous mean to you in your current circumstances? Why are God's promises important to you?

CHAPTER 16

REMEMBER HOW BIG GOD IS, HOW SMALL YOU ARE

Psalm 139:7–12; Jeremiah 32:17; John 10:11–29

QUESTIONS

1. When was a time that you were reminded of how big God is and how small you are? Explain.

2. In a practical sense, does Jesus see us as a big deal or a small deal? Why and how should that affect the way we live?

CHAPTER 17

WE ALL SEE THINGS DIFFERENTLY— AND THAT'S A GOOD THING

Romans 12:6–8; I Corinthians 12:1–11; Ephesians 3:16–21

QUESTIONS

1. How do other people's views and perspectives challenge you in your faith? What is one positive example of how someone has helped you see something differently?

2. How does God's love for you strengthen your courage? How should this shape your thinking and behavior?

CHAPTER 18

IT'S ALL ABOUT PEOPLE, NOT JUST THE EXPERIENCE

Matthew 19:13–15; Luke 10:38–42; Matthew 10:29–31

QUESTIONS

1. Does it fascinate you or frustrate you that others are so different from you? Explain.

2. What does the Bible say about people being important? What impact should that have on us?

CHAPTER 19

OUR PERSPECTIVE IS LIMITED, BUT GOD'S IS NOT

Job 36:22–26; Psalm 25:4–5; Revelation 22:13

QUESTIONS

1. How does having a limited perspective cause you to trust God more and yourself less?

2. How would learning to stay flexible and openhanded with your plans and ideas help you remain open to God's plans?

CHAPTER 20

WHEN YOU GET THROUGH THE TUNNEL, PAY ATTENTION

Proverbs 22:17; Proverbs 27:23; I Chronicles 29:11–12

QUESTIONS

1. Describe a time in your life when you neglected to pay attention to a sign and ended up in a not-so-great place. What would you do differently if you had the chance?

2. How do you describe the greatness of God's majesty and how that should affect the way you live?

CHAPTER 21

OF YOUR HEART

II Kings 6:8–20; Ephesians 1:17–19; Colossians 1:9–12

QUESTIONS

1. Who or what prevents you from seeing the "blue skies" with the "eyes of your heart"?

2. How would asking God to open your eyes to His perspective help you have more hope, peace, joy, and courage?

SPECIAL THANKS . . .

To my wife, Marilyn, and my kids, Nicholas, Abbey, and Jordan, who have joined me on many exciting adventures through the years.

To my grandchildren, Collins, Penn, Brooks, Jase, and Cambree, who are the delight of my life. May you soon discover God's perspective, see His awe and wonder, and enjoy the exciting adventure of surprising joy that He has for your life.

To my parents, Ray and Laurine Barnett, who loved God, loved others, and loved me with a contagious passion that sparked my adventurous spirit.

To my brothers and sisters, especially my sister and brother-in-law, Mary and Randy Boxx, who planned and participated in so many of our wonderful ventures.

To Gini Wietecha, Jason Rovenstine, Kim Marquette, and Marc Hawbaker, for not giving up on the idea of this book, and guiding me with patience and gentleness.

To my teammates across DaySpring through the years, who have encouraged me and allowed me the privilege of serving and living out my faith daily. And to Jane Kisner who has faithfully worked alongside me for more than three decades. Thank you, Jane, for being so genuinely wonderful. You are my hero!

To Ami McConnell, for building a framework for my stories and trips.

To my close friends who have invested in me, especially key mentors along my journey who shaped my life and helped me see with the eyes of my heart to "look again"— Ray Barnett, Robert Cupp, Dean Kerns, Don Leetch, and Steve Menefee.

To every person I've ever known—your life changed my life, because that's what happens—always!

To my Lord and Savior, who has given me life and light along my journey. What a privilege it is to be loved by You!

ABOUT THE AUTHOR

JAMES BARNETT is President of DaySpring, headquartered in Siloam Springs, Arkansas. Founded in 1971, it has been a subsidiary of Hallmark Cards since 1999.

In this role, Barnett leads all aspects of DaySpring's business, overseeing the wholesale and retail operations, including Christian Retail, specialty/mass markets, eCommerce, and Mary & Martha, the company's direct selling division. Under Barnett's leadership, DaySpring has grown to become the world's largest Christian expressions resource provider, annually distributing more than 200 million products throughout the United States and sixty foreign countries. DaySpring touches people over three billion times annually with its physical and digital products. Its employee ministry and service programs support multiple local, national, and global organizations.

Barnett joined DaySpring in 1981, holding key positions within the company in sales and marketing before becoming its leader in 1994. During his tenure, he has led the growth of the DaySpring organization from a small partnership to a thriving multi-national corporation. Barnett is passionate about inspiring and equipping people to know and share God's love. His work at DaySpring allows him to integrate faith and business to fulfill the company's vision to ". . . see every person experience and express the life-changing message of God's love" and to advance its Christian heritage and culture.

Barnett holds a bachelor's degree in business from John Brown University in Siloam Springs, Arkansas, and an MBA from the Walton School of Business at the University of Arkansas in Fayetteville. Barnett resides in Siloam Springs, Arkansas, with his wife Marilyn. The couple has three adult children and five wonderful grandchildren.

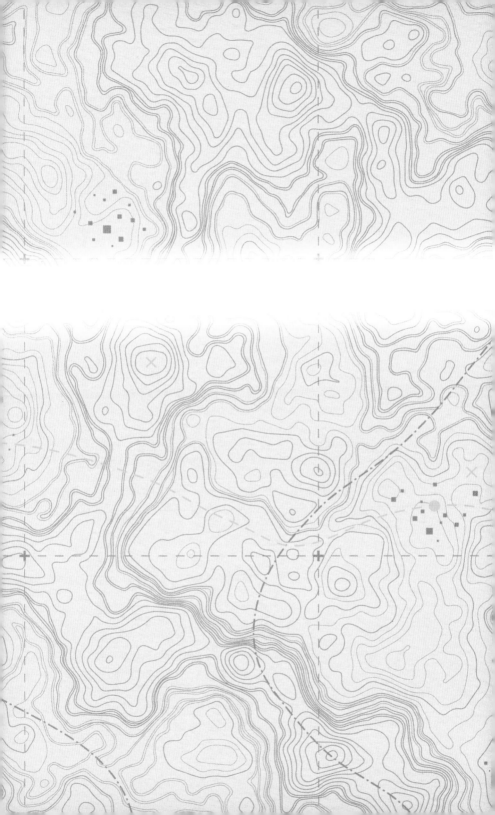